L. LÉPÈRE

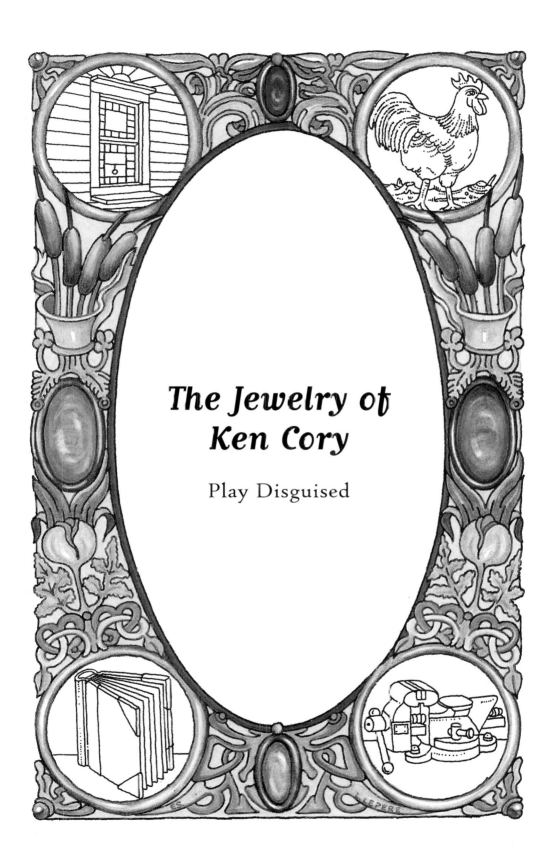

The Jewelry of Ken Cory

Play Disguised

The Jewelry of Ken Cory

Play Disguised

Ben Mitchell

with contributions by Tom Robbins and Nancy Worden

illustrations by Leslie LePere

TACOMA ART MUSEUM

Tacoma Art Museum
in association with
University of Washington Press,
Seattle and London

The Jewelry of Ken Cory: Play Disguised has been published on the occasion of an exhibition and tour organized by the Tacoma Art Museum, which opened in Tacoma September 16 to November 30, 1997.

Exhibition curator: Nancy Worden

ISBN # 0-295-97662-4
Library of Congress #97-61001

Catalogue design: Phil Kovacevich
Editor: Sigrid Asmus
Printed in Hong Kong

Work by Ken Cory is from the estate of the artist unless noted otherwise.

Front and back cover illustrations: *Peanut* (1994); silver, 18K gold, and found object; collection of Louise Kodis

Distributed by the University of Washington Press
P. O. Box 50096
Seattle, WA 98145-5096

Tacoma Art Museum
1123 Pacific Avenue
Tacoma, WA 98402-4399

The Jewelry of Ken Cory: Play Disguised was funded by the estate of the artist.

The Tacoma Art Museum is a membership supported, nonprofit organization. Funding for exhibitions and programs is provided in part by the Tacoma/Pierce County Corporate Council for the Arts, the Forest Foundation, the Institute of Museum Services, the City of Tacoma, and the Washington State Arts Commission.

Contents

Acknowledgments

Ken Cory's work is suspended in fields of tension. Originating in idea—the beginning of all art—it functions as jewelry: portable and wearable objects. Superbly and innovatively made, it is as dense with craft as it is with content. It is animated by the stuff of popular culture while steeped in the exactitude and history of jewelry-making. It is grounded in a regional sense of place—the American West, and specifically the dry, open, intermountain West—but from the beginning it has aimed at a wider range of inquiry. Like Raymond Carver, Richard Hugo, and other recent writers, Cory found the West a fertile resource for images of contemporary America.

With this book and exhibition, the Tacoma Art Museum expands its representation of art in the Northwest. Long committed to collecting, exhibiting, and publishing the work of artists of this region, the Museum here enlarges its mission to encompass metalwork and jewelry. The Northwest, led by Ken Cory and others, has risen to national leadership for narrative or content-based work in this discipline. The Tacoma Art Museum joins a growing number of museums that give contemporary studio jewelry the attention among the arts long granted to handcrafted metalwork in collections of ancient, medieval and non-Western Art.

On behalf of the Museum Board of Trustees and staff, I extend thanks to the many people who contributed to this project. Nancy Worden and Leslie LePere, both long-term friends of Cory's, initiated the exhibition and book. With passion and rigor, Nancy helped ensure that the book stayed true to its subject. Les's drawings enliven the book throughout. Beverly Cory provided essential financial support and wise counsel, making the project possible, and in doing so fulfilled an earlier pledge made by Robert and Susan Cory.

A story such as Ken Cory's begs for a voice that captures the vitality of the person and the intent of the work, that locates the particular within the flow of time and place, and Ben Mitchell proves such a writer, combining incisive assessment with the cadence of a storyteller. Tom Robbins' Foreword starts the book with bull's-eye insight; we are grateful for his contribution. Among the voices woven into the narrative are those of Susan Biskeborn, Jan Brooks, Lane Coulter, Mary Lee Hu, Victor Moore, Gary Noffke, Kiff Slemmons, Ramona Solberg,

Ruth Tamura, Merrily Tompkins, and Lynda Watson-Abbott. Mary Lee Hu also helped resolve questions about the history and techniques of jewelrymaking.

People who have collected Cory's work were generous in agreeing to part with it for the duration of the exhibition and tour. These lenders are Marcella Benditt, Beverly Cory, Helen Drutt English, Daphne Farago, Marion Gartler, Dennis Hadley, Louise Kodis, Les LePere, Jim Manolides, Don Shiffman, Merrily Tompkins, and Nancy Worden.

For the production of the book, photographs of Cory's work were made by Lynn Thompson Hamrick with a keen understanding of jewelry's requirements. The photographs of Cory's house are by Rex Rystadt. Phil Kovacevich provided optimism against the odds and a lively design that builds upon the spirit of Cory's work. Sigrid Asmus provided patient, sensitive, and knowledgeable editing. Nancy and Les wish to add thanks to friends Dick Elliott and Jane Orleman for special kindness and Beth Sellars for cheerleading, as well as to Eva Simova for assistance with illustrations and Ruby Smale for her computer expertise. They join me in thanking my colleagues at the Tacoma Art Museum for their commitment to the project, and for the contribution of their many talents.

The Tacoma Art Museum is pleased once again by the participation of the University of Washington Press in distributing this book, and we thank Pat Soden, director of the Press, for guiding the partnership.

Barbara Johns
Chief Curator, Tacoma Art Museum

Foreword

Tom Robbins

> In a society that is essentially designed to organize, direct, and gratify mass impulses, what is there to minister to the silent zones of man as an individual? Religion? Art? Nature? No, the church has turned religion into standardized public spectacle, and the museum has done the same for art. The Grand Canyon and Niagara Falls have been looked at so much that they've become effete, sucked empty by too many insensitive eyes. What is there to minister to the silent zones of man as an individual? Well, how about a cold chicken bone on a paper plate at midnight, how about a lurid lipstick lengthening or shortening at your command, how about a styrofoam nest abandoned by a "bird" you've never known, how about whitewashed horseshoes crucified like lucky iron Jesuses above a lonely cabin door, how about something beneath a seat touched by your shoe at the movies, how about worn pencils, cute forks, fat little radios, boxes of bow ties, and bubbles on the side of a bathtub? Yes, these are the things, these kite strings and olive oil cans and velvet hearts stuffed with pubic hair, that form the bond between the autistic psyche and the experiential world; it is to show these things in their true mysterious light that is the purpose of the moon.
>
> —*Still Life with Woodpecker* (1980)

Whether Ken Cory ever read the preceding lines, or if so, whether he completely agreed with them, we cannot know. It is certain, however, that he would have understood them. The relationship between humanity and so-called lifeless objects is often more complex and enigmatic than the connection between humanity and nature. In the shifting psychological shadows of the organic/inorganic trellis, Cory tended his grapes and pressed his wine.

Many of us feel trapped, oppressed, compromised by the excess of material goods that surround and sometimes beleaguer us. Yet, despite our expressed intention to simplify our existence, we continue to amass objects of all uses and sizes—to save us time, bolster our status, extend our egos, or insulate us falsely against the approaching December of death. The possibility that the things themselves might possess a personality, an energy, a matrix of meaning beyond the pragmatic, beyond the symbolic, beyond the totemic, beyond the aesthetic, even, is a notion that normally eludes us. Apparently, it did not elude Ken Cory.

If art deals with the philosophy of life, and craft with the philosophy of materials, Cory—like one of those sweet pink dumb phallic erasers he admired—scuffed out the line between the two (much as, on a more specific level, he blurred the boundary between elegance and funk).

His ornaments have been called "tiny sculptures," but that seems not quite exact. They are too theatrical, too narrative, to fit any formalist definition of sculpture. More accurately, they are tiny tableaus. A Cory creation may function as a pin, an ashtray, or a buckle, but what he has actually produced is a miniature environment. He constructed little worlds. And in those small worlds he made his secret home.

If the objects and images he so meticulously fashioned and fervently collected reflect his personal proclivities, they also, simultaneously, reveal the hidden character of the things themselves. In other words, Cory did not merely endow his pieces with humor, bawdiness, poetry, vitality, beauty, and mystery, he had the vision to recognize that those qualities were implicit in the "objective" materials all along.

Like the ancients, Ken Cory moved in a divinely animated universe—animated even when it was static and mute, divine even when it was goofy and crass.

Drawn to junkyards, garage sales, and hardware stores the way a mystic is drawn to a mountaintop, a satyr to a rutting ground, or a beekeeper to a hive, Cory clearly *needed* the theater of objecthood. Perhaps it needed him, as well.

—March 1997

Introduction

Nancy Worden

> Who says paintings aren't functional? That big abstract that was hanging in the stairway by where you kept your bike has proved to be quite useful. It was one of the things that didn't sell in the yard sale so I took it off the stretcher bars because I needed the boards. So then I had this big piece of canvas that I decided would make a great tarp to lay on when I am working under my car. It works just great! Also I use it under my sleeping bag. The paint makes it waterproof and when it gets dirty I can just hose it off and the abstract shapes harmonize nicely with the natural environment. It's the prettiest tarp I've ever seen. Form follows function.

This excerpt from a letter written to me in the summer of 1979 best conveys the kind of humor and sarcasm that Ken Cory maintained about art and life, and for him art and life were one and the same. For three decades he created objects that were simple yet profound, archetypal as well as contemporary, iconoclastic and classic at the same time. Although he cared about craftsmanship and quality, he never let technique preside over ideas. Visually and intellectually, he kept us on our toes.

Ken Cory's studio, with rolling mill, 1994

When Ken died, Les LePere and I had the same response: we wanted to create a book and exhibition about Ken and his art to give his work greater exposure. What started as a labor of love evolved into a larger mission—to provide not only a history of his personal journey, but also a glimpse of the big picture, the contribution he made to American studio jewelry. Ken's work was recognized and published steadily from 1967 on. He gained attention at a very early age, and most authors have categorized him either by his early Funk work from the late 1960s or by the graphic work of the Pencil Brothers era. The work he produced from 1978 to 1994 has not been widely published or shown. He was never a good self-promoter, and after the Summervail workshops ended in the mid-1980s he gradually lost touch with many of his professional peers. He hated selling his work and kept most of the pieces for himself instead of releasing them to private or public collections where they would have received more recognition.

One of the many challenges of this project was establishing titles for the work. Most of Ken's early pieces were untitled, while the later ones had nicknames, and sometimes more than one. Many of the titles used in this book were fabricated by Les LePere and me for purely practical reasons; it was either that or give them all a number. If Ken gave a piece a title, we have used it; when he didn't and we assigned one, the word "Untitled" appears in the caption for its illustration. To assist readers to find the page where a particular piece is illustrated—this includes other artists' work also—we have added an Index of Illustrations at the back of the book.

Another challenge was the puzzle of recent metalsmithing history and terminology. Because the field is just beginning to be documented, we bumped into jewelry design movements that had no labels—for example, the period dating roughly from the late 1950s through the early 1970s. Ken called it "Snot Jewelry," Mary Hu refers to it as "Wax in the Water," and Lane Coulter jokingly describes it as the "Drippy Wax and Baroque Pearl Period." It paralleled the Beat movement and Abstract Expressionism in painting, but it has no "official" art-historical name. It was a time of giddy exploration with primitive techniques, like pouring hot wax into snow or water and casting it, or burning holes in sheet metal with a torch. The results of these experiments were nonobjective, organic blobs that might be hung on a leather thong as a pendant. These freeform artifacts look crude to us now, but making jewelry *as art* was an exciting new concept then. While swirly, stone-laden designs were still alive and well in the commercial jewelry trade, American designer craftsmen at that time were deliberately trying to break away from those stereotypes and to align themselves with what was happening in painting and sculpture.

The nature and value of Ken's contribution to American art jewelry also sparked some lively discussions. In November of 1996, jewelers Ramona Solberg, Mary Hu, and I met with writer Ben Mitchell to look at Ken's work and discuss its evolution and imagery. Ramona contributed a key insight: because there was no jewelry program at Washington State University when Ken was in graduate school there, he worked with the sculptor George Laisner. This made Ken's experience very different from the one he might have had at a school with a traditional metalsmithing program. Later, during the Summervail workshops, he became passionately involved with traditional jewelry techniques and materials and incorporated them in his work. However, Ken always maintained that his work was small sculpture. I think Ramona's observation is an important one; it points to the freedom that enabled him to find and develop his unique imagery so early.

Mary Hu offered another important insight: his strong interest in a sense of place. At a time when the work of most American jewelry artists maintained clear aesthetic ties to a particular school or mentor, Ken managed to absorb the essence of the *culture* he lived in, providing a perspective that was American, western, rural, and male. For example, his big belt buckles were right in line with men's fashions in the 1970s, and especially so in the cattle-raising community where he lived and taught. Ellensburg is famous for its annual Labor Day rodeo, and distinctive belt buckles, awarded as trophies to winners of rodeo events all over the west, are part of the standard cowboy uniform.

We also spent a lot of time looking at and talking about his collections. Ken made regular, weekly pilgrimages to the junk stores in Ellensburg and Yakima, and his house was an organized museum of his "finds." He was a collector of collections: I don't think he owned just one of anything. For Ken, collecting was research. The objects were an encyclopedia of his visual language and directly related to the images and techniques he used in his artwork.

One example of the relationship of his collections to his artwork is champlevé enameling. (Champlevé and other metalworking techniques

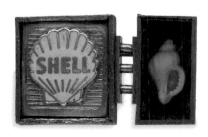

Shell (pin). 1970
Copper, silver, enamel, cast resin, and shell
1 × 1½ × ½ in.

Brick Breast Bottle (female side), 1971
Cast copper, enamel, silver, brass,
and cork
2 × 1¼ × 1 in.

Brick Breast Bottle (male side), 1971
Cast copper, silver, and cork
2 × 1¼ × 1 in.

are explained in the Glossary.) In talking about Ken's enamel work, Mary Hu asked me, "Where did it come from?" Few in American studio jewelry were using this process before he did. Ken collected emblematic jewelry—like the lowly bowling league pins and company tie-tacks that the commercial jewelry industry has been making for decades. The first evidence of this process shows up in *Shell*, of 1970, a miniature version of the famous petroleum company logo, and he used the technique frequently in his work after that. His collection of enameled signs, with their distinctive hard-edge outlining, was another strong influence.

An interest in Chinese cloisonné snuff bottles inspired *Brick Breast Bottle*, of 1971. Many of the bottles in Ken's personal collection are flat on two sides; all have images on the front and back, and round, domed lids that hold a stopper and a paddle-shaped scoop. *Brick Breast Bottle* is not only a snuff bottle, it illustrates the yin/yang, hard/soft idea of brick breasts that the Pencil Brothers had fun with in their Pullman days. One side of the bottle is female, the other side is definitely male. The work is part of a metalsmithing tradition that goes way back and is present in many cultures—the making of small, decorated containers for holding snuff, tobacco, spices, and makeup, and the decoration of other small functional objects.

Ken also admired the beautiful beadwork of the nearby Yakima Indian tribe and collected Plateau Indian beaded bags, often incorporating some of their naïve style in his work. Naturalistic imagery like this exemplifies the kind of folk art he liked to look at, and relates to the Grange displays he documented at the Western Washington State Fair. Every year each Grange or regional branch of The Patrons of Husbandry shows off their particular harvest specialties in unique arrangements—apples carefully patterned with ears of corn, or stalks of wheat, or whatever they produce. Juried by visitors to the fair, the displays inspire their designers to adventurous creations with animals, complex patterns, or even narrative scenes. He never lost his love of the Grange displays, and his admiration for other folk art forms. For example, he used the humble bean mosaic to create the sophisticated yet smart-alecky and iconoclastic *Portrait of Chairman Mao Bean Mosaic* in 1977. *Mao* is a kindred spirit to *Fuck You Lady Said the Parrot* (1976) and *What Is the Point of This Piece* (1973), two humorous belt buckles the Pencil Brothers created to deliberately shock and offend people.

Ken was always resurrecting techniques that his peers had written off as "too dumb" to bother with. The best example is *101 Twisted Wires*, a piece that he began in 1979 as both an academic exercise and a personal challenge. At a time when most of his peers were focused on elaborate high-tech methods in metalsmithing, Ken turned to something extremely simple: How many

Portrait of Chairman Mao Bean Mosaic, 1977
Dried beans, glue, and wood
3 ft. × 2 ft. × 1 in. approx.
Whereabouts unknown

Grange display, late 1970s
Apples, beans, corn, eggs, and related items

ways can you twist a wire? To find the answer, Ken used many of the fifty drawplates he owned; he could make any gauge of triangular, square, half-round, hexagonal, oval, or even star-shaped wire. *101 Twisted Wires* is a conceptual as well as a technical masterpiece, an achievement that is an extension of his love of pattern and collecting.

Jeweler's Loupe with Stamped Designs,
1985
Sterling silver and glass
1½ × 1 × ½ in.
Collection of Beverly Cory

Set of Design Stamps, ca. 1977–1990
High-carbon steel
Largest, 3½ × 1 in.; smallest, 2½ × ³⁄₁₆ × ¼ in.
Collection of Nancy Worden

Homemade drawplates
Triangular Drawplate, 1978; high-carbon steel;
14 × 1¼ × ¼ in.
Star Drawplate, 1978; high-carbon steel;
12¼ × 1 ⅛ × ¼ in.
Heart Drawplate, 1979; high-carbon steel;
9 × 1½ × ¼ in.
Collection of Nancy Worden

During the late 1970s and early 1980s, Ken was almost totally immersed in this kind of investigative research. He combined it with toolmaking, another old metalsmithing tradition, and made many of his own tools. For instance, he designed and made a tool that he called the "Coryograph" for inscribing repetitive patterns on metal, the kind of wavy or spiraling patterns you see on the inside of old watch cases. His intention was to use the patterns behind transparent enamels, known as the basse-taille process. Other handmade tools were three drawplates made from old truck springs and a number of decorative stamps he made from steel files. These stamps were created to make the elegant patterns that often appear on the pins he made from 1985 to 1993; others are recognizable images of birds, cars, snakes, and so on, and showed up as hallmarks on the back of a work or on gifts he made for his family and friends.

While many contemporary metalsmiths have made their reputations by exploring a single technique, Ken always chose the technique that best suited his imagery. An example is the use of granulation for the tongue on the paperweight, *Monument to Katie Moon*. This is a very complex technique to learn for the sake of one or two situations. Another example of a "dumb" process he used, rarely but effectively, was cuttlefish bone casting. Carving and then casting in this medium results in characteristic wavy ridges that are perfectly suited to the topographical images in *Ring Toss Box* from 1972, and that appear again in one of his last pieces, nicknamed *Beach*, from 1993. Finally, Ken's last works provide many examples of masonite die-forming. This simple low-tech process was used to push a "puffed" relief into pieces like *Coffee* (1987), *Arm* (1988), and *Dress* (1988).

(Untitled) Ring Toss Box, 1972
Copper, 18K gold, and silver
1¼ × 1½ × 1¼ in.

Ken made rings intermittently over the years, primarily for himself. Rings are always a special problem for a jewelry designer: a ring has to be able to withstand a lot of abuse and be comfortable to wear, yet the stage is so small that a lot of art jewelers avoid them. There just isn't much space or freedom for imagery. Ken's rings always reflected in miniature the imagery he was exploring in his larger pieces.

(Untitled) Space Ship Ring,
1973
18K gold and star sapphire
1¼ × 1 × ½ in.

From 1980 and continuing to the last year of his life, Ken was working on a set of cards, similar in format to Tarot cards. These cards were originally conceived back in the heyday of the Pencil Brothers; Ken and Les designed the reverse side together and had a set of a hundred printed up for each of them, leaving the "face" side blank. Ken's designs for his set of cards are a visual inventory of the "100 Essential Images" that he used over and over in his work. These are the images that open each section of Ben Mitchell's essay.

Ken's world, although it was filled with tools, contained very little modern technology. He had a car and a radio, but never owned a TV set, a vacuum cleaner, or a

(Untitled) Arch Ring, ca. 1968
Copper and 14K gold
1¼ × ¾ × ¼ in.

Ken Cory at fountain in Pioneer Square, Seattle 1973

washing machine. He was a perfectionist and a careful observer who always carried a jeweler's loupe in his pocket. He was not a snob about his intelligence or education and rated people on their ability to tell a good story. He was a good listener in a time when this has become a lost art. He could drive a thousand miles or more to see an art show and then just turn around and come back. He would put as much effort into baking a cake for George Washington's birthday or designing a toy boat as he did into any of his art pieces. He had his own rules about life, some of which are permanently etched on my brain:

1. Always take the scenic route.

2. Never leave the house without your sketchbook and camera.

3. Beware of people who take themselves too seriously.

4. Make the back look as good as the front.

5. Why buy something when you can have the fun of making it yourself?

In the summer of 1993, the Washington State Arts Commission asked a select group of jewelry artists to submit slides and an artist's statement for consideration for a large commission. This is the statement Ken Cory submitted:

I invoke my Fifth Amendment right to remain silent in order to avoid self-incrimination.

The patch where I pick blackberries every fall has the biggest, sweetest, most plentiful berries I have ever seen. A Yakima Indian who picks in the same area told me this was the best picking that he had ever seen and that he had picked berries throughout the Cascades from up in Canada to down in Oregon. I've wondered what it is that makes these berries so much better than all the others. Is it because of the amount of sun that hits this field, or is it the soil, or the prevailing wind, or the moisture that accumulates here? I don't know why it is. All I need to know is that the berries are good and the picking is fast.

I think that we have in recent years forgotten the primary function of jewelry which is, of course, to communicate with folks from other planets in other solar systems. Anyone wearing one of my badges will have nothing to fear when we are invaded from outer space.

The commission went to someone else, but we are left with this gift in Ken's voice. His statement makes us wonder if he's just fooling around or if maybe he's smarter than we are and there is some profound metaphor hidden there for those clever enough to decode it. He always avoided the obvious and challenged his audience to figure it out for themselves. Ultimately, Ken's legacy is more than his words or the objects he made: It is a philosophy about *making*. For him, making art had nothing to do with money, academic politics, having shows, or being famous. For him, making art was about life, death, love, hate, sex, communicating with other human beings, and the joy of making stuff. He personified an adventurous, uninhibited, playful spirit that American studio jewelry has lost along the road to its maturity.

Dear Nancy,

Well here I am back from Vail. What a trip. My car worked perfectly on the entire trip except for one event, the cause of which, I can only attribute to Indian spirits who must have been testing my injunuity. It happened in Chaco Canyon forty miles from the nearest paved road out on the New Mexico desert. It's an area where there are a number of pueblo ruins. Just as I entered the canyon my muffler fell off. While I was wiring it back on a tire went flat. After I changed the tire the car wouldn't start because the battery was dead because the fan belt was too loose. I pushed the car and got it started and decided to leave it running while I explored a pueblo ruin. When I returned the radiator had boiled and one of the hoses was broken and the water was squirting out. All this happened in 104 degree heat. But I solved the problems so I guess I passed the test.

—Ken Cory letter, 1980

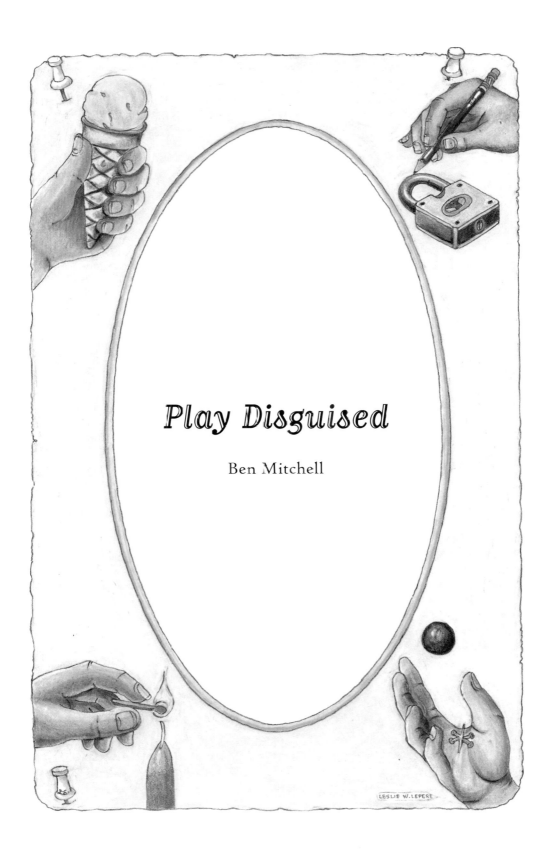

Play Disguised

Ben Mitchell

Ken Cory, 1989

Blackbird, Fly
Ellensburg, Washington, January 16, 1994

Ken Cory died too young, of diabetes-induced heart failure, at only fifty, sometime while he slept during the night of January 16, 1994. Among the work that he left behind in his Ellensburg home and studio was a shelf of more than two dozen sketchbooks. Each one is an identical size—five and a half by eight and a half inches—and has a black cover. Each had been carefully, sequentially hand-numbered by Cory at the upper spine on a neat, red-edged label protected with clear household tape. Several blank sketchbooks were on the shelf, numbered and ready to use.

There are many themes and motifs in the life and work of Ken Cory: his seemingly boundless inventiveness and openness to the possibilities of his chosen materials and tools; his love of beautiful women and a small, fast car; the long road trips he took throughout his adult life; his spontaneous, infectious, generous laugh, prankster-like playfulness, and bawdy good humor; the provocations and challenges he fired off, through his work, to the crafts community from the late 1960s through the mid-1990s; his returning, again and again, to the Yakima River Canyon south of his small house in Ellensburg to walk and camp and make love and fashion with friends spontaneous art out of wire and found objects that they left behind there in the arroyos and along the banks of the creeks and river; his enduring reclusiveness. His collections, dozens and dozens of collections: pencils, beads, toys, Columbia Plateau beaded bags, board games, enameled signs, palindromes, bottles, tools, stones. The foundation for his research, the collections represent Ken Cory's lifelong fascination with and exploration of the *object* and the *image*—in his life, in his art, and in the American culture which he addressed through his jewelry.

Between 1967, when as a student he made those early, remarkable pins— *Tongue, Nipple, Wave, Beads*—out of cast silver, cast and electroformed copper, glass, plastic, and leather, and 1994, when he fabricated what would be his last pin, *Peanut*, Ken Cory had, along with early Funk and Pop jewelers Fred Woell, Robert Ebendorf, Don Tompkins, and some of his more immediate peers, fundamentally changed the ways we now approach the materials and traditions out of which American art jewelry is made. These metalsmiths, with Ken Cory's unique vision

Details from Ken Cory's collections, 1994
Top: miniature cast-iron frying pans and brass
hose nozzles; Bottom: a selection of toys.

central in the movement after the late 1960s, changed not only the way we view metalsmithing and jewelry, but also their place in our day-to-day lives. His contributions to American craft and to jewelry are enormous.

He was called a Funk artist, a "narrative" jeweler. He was both and neither. Though traditionally trained —with a Bachelor of Fine Arts in Metal from Oakland's California College of Arts and Crafts and a Master of Fine Arts in Jewelry from Washington State University (WSU) in Pullman—he was an autodidact, an iconoclast. A gregarious and fun-loving man with a small, close-knit community of friends and colleagues, he was at the same time a deeply private man who lived alone. A master craftsman and a bold experimenter— he created the tool if there was no tool at hand to do the task he wished. A generous, demanding, and gifted teacher. Riding his bicycle the short distance to campus to teach. Going off on his annual summer road trips in his beloved MG, revisiting the canyons and mountains, the cliff dwellings, pueblos, and national parks that his family had visited each summer he was growing up. Corresponding with his closest friends. Visiting and caring for his parents in Ellensburg where, in their later years, he had encouraged them to buy a home close to him. In the last decade of his life he was Crusoe in Ellensburg, living quietly and simply, filling those dozens of sketchbooks with project ideas, researching metalsmithing techniques and materials in the old out-of-print how-to manuals he loved so much, sometimes making his own clothes, designing and building tools, putting together his collections. Experimenting with innumerable processes and materials. Working, always working.

Roadmap

The Work, 1963–1994

Cory's work as an artist falls rather neatly into four major periods. First, his earliest jewelry from 1967 through 1971, which received virtually immediate attention in the metal-smithing and crafts community, produced when he was a graduate student and in the few years following his gradua-tion. Second, the period from about 1971 through 1979, in which he explored narrative-based jewelry, enameled func-tional objects, and engaged in the collaboration with Les LePere, which they called "The Pencil Brothers." Third, between the late 1970s and 1986-87, a deeply intro-spective period when he made very little jewelry. And between 1986 and 1994, his last work.

The earliest significant works are *Tongue, Beads, Wave, Reflector, Black and White,* and *Nipple,* from 1967; *Pin* (the piece that so many of his peers saw in the 1970 *Objects USA* catalogue), *Zipper, Red Snake, Hose,* and *Drain* from 1968; *Shift* from 1969; *Levers, Shell,* and *Sword* from 1970; *Window Box, Brick Breast Bottle, Rope,* and the wonderful-ly eccentric, mysterious *Monument to Katie Moon,* all from 1971. This first wave of work, begun when Cory was twenty-four years old and com-pleted before he was yet thirty, is astounding enough technically, but is all the more significant for its singu-lar mastery of the vernacular, and for the depth and freshness of its imagi-native vision. It is, from the begin-ning, fully original work.

(Untitled) Black and White (pin), 1967
Copper and plastic
2 × 1¾ × ½ in.

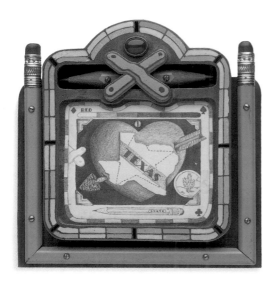

PENCIL BROTHERS
Texas (wall piece), 1972
Enamel on copper, glass, carnelian, graphite drawing,
and pencils
4 × 4 × ¾ in.
Collection of Daphne Farago

The second group of work, roughly from 1971 through 1979, encompasses objects made by the Pencil Brothers, when Cory worked in partnership with his good friend from WSU graduate school, the artist and graphic designer Les LePere, as well as the pieces Cory produced independently of the collaboration. Works from this time include the Pencil Brothers' *Camel* and *Train* from 1971; *Texas* from 1972; the *Bird* and *Fish* pendants for the "Pencil Sisters" from 1974; several switchplates like *Frame* from 1975; the ashtray *Match* from 1976, and the 1977 wall piece, *Skunk*. During this same period, Cory made *Broken Window* in 1972; and a funny, fascinating series of works resonant of the history and traditions of American Indian metalsmithing, including *Squash Blossom Necklace*, *TIN NUTS*, and *Autumn Sunset (Candy Corn)*, all in 1974 and 1975; and the whimsical *Self Portrait* and emblematic *Flats Fixed* and *Mix-n-Match* buckles in 1975. Then, in one amazing burst in 1976, he produced what would be the last group of graphic, narrative-based belt buckles: *High Heel*, *Admit One*, *Field*, *How to Fix Your Snake*, and *Route 66*; followed by the *Portrait of Chairman Mao Bean Mosaic* in 1977. This second period—so varied, complex, and fundamental in Cory's aesthetic development—encompassed the dynamic partnership with LePere, an exploration of the narrative and graphic potential in jewelry. It displays an interest in the popular and emblematic imagery of American consumer culture, an often trenchant and satiric send-up of dominant social and cultural norms, a deep study of several American Indian metalsmithing and iconographic traditions, and the broadening of a sophisticated sense of humor.

The third period is complex and problematic. Between roughly the late 1970s and 1986 Cory made very little finished jewelry. There are a number of fascinating and compelling pieces from this period, including *Nancy's Buckle*, the *101 Twisted*

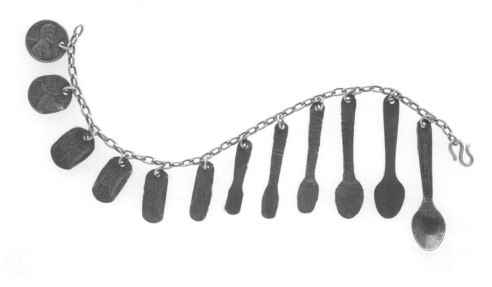

Metamorphosis (bracelet), 1981
Copper and silver
9 × 2½ × ¼ in.

Wires, and *Metamorphosis*, but these years may be best understood as a time of introspection, of aesthetic and technical play and inquiry. A time for experiment, for reflection, and research, as he prepared for the next, and what would be the last, major group of ideas and works During this period he was working on his house and annually making gifts for his family and friends—pencil sharpeners, cookie cutters, all kinds of functional objects. Works from this period that deserve our attention here include 1978's *Strike It Rich* and *Beautiful Lady*, that continue his investigation of traditional American Indian jewelry techniques; two new pieces, *Nancy's Buckle* in 1978 and the pin *V8* in 1979; his full-sized, hand-carved *Wooden Table*, which he made for and used in his home, *Cupcake Box*, and *Tape Measure*, all in 1980; *101 Twisted Wires* (1979-81); and the 1981 bracelet, *Metamorphosis*, a pivotal piece, a transition or bridge to what would follow.

Between 1986 and his death in 1994 he made twenty-one pins. This work appears to move in a completely different direction from all that had come before. It more closely adheres to traditional jewelers' materials and techniques, incorporating 18 and 24K gold, sterling silver, copper, and oddly cut semiprecious stones. The forms in these last works are more refined than the earlier cast-copper, electroformed and enameled pieces and the Pencil Brothers works. This work seems more abstract, dense, private, more in the spirit of high than low aesthetics. But it

Boat (pin), 1987
Silver, 18K gold, and garnet
1 × 2 × ½ in.

really isn't, as we'll see looking at it more closely. The best of the last works include the breakthrough piece from 1986, *Face*; *Arm, Bear, Coffee, Boat,* and *Table* from 1987; *Sign, Whip, Fire, Landscape, Saw, Tent,* and *Dress* from the hugely fertile 1988; *Arches* from 1990; *Knows* and *Satellite* in 1991; *Beach* in 1993; and last, *Peanut*, completed just before his death. One thing stands out here: the aesthetic and intellectual links between these last works and his earliest work from 1967 to 1971. Tracing the contrasts between, say, the pin *Wave* made in 1967, and the pin *Landscape* made just a few years before his death, or between the 1971 *Rope* and the 1988 *Whip*, we find in the last works a transcendence, on both the aesthetic and technical levels, of his earliest explorations. At the same time, these final pins are fully grounded, in content and intention, in his earliest, boldly individualistic explorations in cast copper and plastic. There is a masterful fusion of qualities. Low and high culture meet here in an aesthetic that seems to effortlessly contain images from both popular culture and art-historical sources. Jewelry, with its long history of craft and decoration, is in his last work transformed, through a surprisingly postmodernist sensibility, into a deeply imaginative, personal iconography.

"Good science consists largely of play disguised as serious work," Cory wrote in his Sketchbook Number 23 sometime soon after March 1990. His life and his art were play disguised. His last work is an interrupted inquiry. Unfinished or not, these last pieces are provocative and compelling—and hauntingly beautiful. At the end, Cory returned to two distinct sets of roots in his art: the long, rich tradition of jewelry-making, with its infinite potential for creating the image in metal and stone, and the vocabulary of his own strong imaginative vision.

Rural Route

Pullman, Washington 1945–1963

Cory was born in Kirkland, Washington, in 1943, where his father, Robert, worked as a radio electrician in the Lake Washington Shipyards during the war. In 1945 Robert Cory moved his small family—his wife Susan and their two-year-old son Kenneth—to Pullman, Washington, in the dry, rolling Palouse Hills country on the far eastern edge of the state, where Robert took a position as an instructor in chemistry at Washington State College (now Washington State University). Ken Cory's entire childhood was spent in Pullman. He left in 1963 to study at the California College of Arts and Crafts in Oakland, then returned to Pullman to complete his M.F.A. at WSU. He taught for a single year at CCAC in 1971 before being hired by Central Washington State College (also now University) the following year. He lived for the rest of his life in a small house on 14th Street in Ellensburg, Washington—that sleepy, central Washington ranch and university town at the foot of the eastern Cascades in the Kittitas Valley—leaving each summer for long road trips, spending some weeks at the Summervail metalsmithing conferences in Vail, Colorado, from 1975 through 1984, teaching, filling the sketchbooks, searching through junk stores and flea markets, working with metal.

In all artists' lives, the twin geographies of childhood, that is, both the *exterior* and *interior* geographies, are the primary forces that permanently shape the artist's dominant themes and images. Ken Cory is no exception. Cory's sister, Beverly Cory, an editor now living in the San Francisco Bay Area, was born in Pullman in 1947. She recounts, in wonderful detail, how it was to grow up there—the nature of their family, its quirkiness and delightful eccentricity, life in the

Ken Cory, age six, 1950

"Once—I think Cory was in junior high about this time," Victor Moore remembers, "the family was on one of their summer trips in the southwest. Their car broke down somewhere way back on a dirt road in the New Mexico or California desert. They'd busted a tie rod. Robert Cory got the family all set up in the shade on a blanket with some lunch, took out the spare tire, and by cutting pieces off the tire's sidewall with his pocket knife, somehow riveted the pieces together—he must have had one of those home rivet guns with him—and made a handmade tie rod, installed it on the car, and limped the car to the nearest town, more than fifty miles away over a bad road."

There are many similar stories from Ken Cory's young years. It is certain that he was always watching Robert closely.

nuclear family during the repressed and prudish America of the 1950s, the textures and tones of eastern Washington's small-town university life. And, as Beverly Cory's memories and stories make clear, Robert Cory, a sometimes severe, laconic but witty, wholly independent, wonderfully odd man and father, played a central role in shaping his son's personality, and thus his art. Beverly Cory's stories[1] are the place to begin on the way to understanding Ken Cory's later life and art.

"While we were growing up," Beverly Cory says, "Pullman had a population of about four or five thousand. It was a sleepy little town, even with the college, and in the summer when the college kids were gone, it was practically comatose. The college was largely an agricultural and veterinarian school—it had long been termed a 'cow college.' So there wasn't a lot of culture."

Not long after the move to Pullman, Robert Cory left the Chemistry Department for a research position in plant physiology with the Botany Department. Primarily he studied the effects of radiation on plants. Beverly Cory says, "It's safe to say that what he did for a living was not where his heart was; his heart instead was in his enormous garden, in the woodworking he did around the house, and in the travels he took us on every summer."

Robert Cory was an intense and unusual man. Beverly Cory remembers: "Among the things that surely made him an eccentric in small-town Pullman was that when we were young he wasn't one to socialize with the neighbors, even casually. He never had a car newer than ten years old—this in a era when the norm was to buy a new model every few years. And he never used the car around town, insisting we could walk." Rather than two weeks at the lake, Robert Cory took his family on long car trips each summer. There was no phone or television in the house until the kids were in high school. He was a vegetarian, "Virtually unheard of in those days," Beverly Cory says. He was extremely frugal—thanks to Scotch ancestry and the Depression—and drove the seventy miles to Spokane to shop or ordered from catalogs rather than buy from local stores. He never threw anything out, and the house and yard and the old shed out back were filled with all the things he saved.

In 1951 Robert bought the home Ken and Beverly would grow up in, a tiny frame house, alongside three adjacent vacant lots on Pioneer Hill, a site from which the family could look across the town to the campus on College Hill. Robert Cory spent years working on the house himself, expanding it, changing it. Ken Cory's house in Ellensburg, the house that he died in, would also be very small and carefully cared for.

They were a family who worked hard, who made things, who fixed things, who made do with what was at hand. Susan Cory sewed all the curtains and drapes for the house, painted all the house siding and trim, cooked, baked, made

Beverly and Ken Cory, Disneyland, 1956

candy, canned vegetables and fruits from the huge Cory garden, and sewed many of her own and the children's clothes as well. She made shirts for Ken long after he was grown. Beverly remembers, "She would stick a single teasel or bunch of delicate dried grasses in a small ceramic pot or vase and place it 'just so' in a window to very nice effect. The message I got was 'do it cheap and do it right'—and that even went for art. A relative once gave us a set of flower pictures, botanically accurate, to be painted with watercolors. We were forbidden to paint them until we could do it 'right' according to what the flowers really looked like. Consequently they sat in the closet untouched forevermore. Another time we were both given sketchbooks and told quite firmly that these were to be used only for sketching the real things we saw before us, not for 'just drawing.'" A born artist, Ken knew when to rebel: at painting by number. "While I faithfully filled in my paint-by-number picture, color by color and numbered space by numbered space, Ken took the tiny pots of oil paint, mixed his own

33

colors, and created his own weird and wonderful abstract painting on the given board, totally ignoring the intended purpose.

"Ken was always deliberate and exacting in all things he did. His hobby as a child was building plastic model cars, many of them 'antique.' He had an obsession with cars and would spend hours sketching them, their fins, fenders, grills, hood ornaments, the 'flames' that were part of customizing jobs. When he got his first car—a '57 Plymouth purchased secondhand from an uncle, after he graduated from high school—he didn't add flames but he did paint it and sewed his own 'tuck-and-roll' black upholstery.

"Small scale, it occurs to me, was a recurring theme: small worlds for his little cars in the sandbox and for his electric train. Little cabins of Lincoln Logs, little buildings of white plastic bricks. The little cardboard buildings for a whole town that he made from the cut-out-and-fold-up patterns printed on those Shredded Wheat boxes. The small-scale model cars. On one camping trip we visited the Anasazi cave dwellings at Mesa Verde. We were camped out in the desert at the base of a huge rock cliff and Ken built his own small-scale cave dwelling into the side of the cliff with pebbles and mud."

The issue of scale in Cory's art—what it is and how it works—is a theme which reverberates throughout this narrative. When I first had the opportunity to see virtually all of Cory's life's work in jewelry and fabricated objects, it all fit in a few cases and boxes on a dining room table.

Window Box (pin), 1971
Cast silver, copper, brass, sodalite, glass, and enamel
2½ × 1¼ × 1¼ in.

Other than his immediate family, there was no one more important to Cory in his early life and development as an artist than Victor Moore, his art teacher from grade school through high school graduation. In a rather remarkable bit of serendipity, when Cory returned to Pullman from Oakland in 1967 to take his M.F.A. at Washington State University, Victor Moore, having returned to school, was also working on an M.F.A. in the WSU Art Department. Though separated by a generation, the teacher and the student were now peers. Moore, like

Robert Cory, was also something of an oddity in Pullman. The Pullman school administration had a dress code for its teachers during the 1950s and 60s, calling for all men to wear neckties. Instead, Moore didn't shave his neck hair in front, but let it grow long like a beard, braided it, and wore it as a "hair tie." He was, in Beverly Cory's words again, "a colorful, flamboyant character in Pullman, and this appealed to Ken and I think gave him a role model for his later life."

Victor Moore had a profound and enduring influence on Cory's life and work. He early recognized Cory's gifts and encouraged him, tutored him, and challenged him. Listening to Moore talk today, one realizes how delighted he was

Victor Moore's "Castle," 1970
Pullman, Washington

with his young student's keen awareness, his technical and imaginative gifts, his early love of art. Theirs was a long and remarkable relationship. Significantly, Moore also stimulated and encouraged Cory's lifelong love for mining small-town junk stores and flea markets for treasures and ideas to incorporate into his art. Ken Cory and Victor Moore remained friends throughout Cory's life.

Victor Moore remembers two fundamentally important aspects of the young Ken Cory. First, his natural talent and curiosity about art and the world around him. "'Cory' [as Moore affectionately referred to Ken Cory throughout our talks] mastered all the techniques of drawing on his own. When I was teaching, I always required out-of-class sketchbooks. His were always a joy to see. He would do shapes that he'd want to use in pottery [Cory went to CCAC intending to study ceramics]. He'd do sketches from real life, from odd things, from everything. But it wasn't just in art that he was talented, he was curious and smart and good at everything that interested him. For instance, once he decided to ride his bicycle to Seattle [a trip of over 200 miles including crossing Snoqualmie Pass in the Cascade Range], and he *did* it."

One year, this would have been Cory's junior year in high school I think, at the beginning of school I noticed that Cory wasn't in my class. I thought it was strange, but I didn't ponder on it. One day, well into the fall, I got this letter from England:

> Dear Mr. Moore,
> I have been traveling through Europe speaking against the effects of alcohol. As an example to my audiences, I have with me a drunk named Tom. Yesterday Tom died. I am writing to ask you to take his place.
>> Yours,
>> John Colt

I learned later that the Cory family's summer trip had been to Africa, by tramp steamer. The family hated the freighter, so Robert and Susan changed plans to return on it, and went through Africa, across Europe and home across the North Atlantic in late October on the *Queen Elizabeth II*. I always knew Cory wrote me that letter, but he never said a word to me about it all those years.

—Victor Moore

Another factor that figures largely in Cory's personality and work, and which Victor Moore remembers well, both from Cory's school years and from the time they were completing their M.F.A. work together, is Cory's penchant for pranks, jokes, and gags. "Capers," Moore calls them. "He was too bright to ever get caught," Moore says. "I could almost condone his pranks they were so good." And while they are too numerous to recount here, one in particular bears telling.

"We were in graduate school together," Victor Moore remembers, "housed in an old fire station as a temporary art department while a new building was under construction. Each graduate student could pick a room for his studio. There were lots of rooms. There was even one great big room with a foundry in it and everything. And there was a broom closet. Guess who took the broom closet? And do you know, it looked just like his house in Ellensburg. Now, also at this time they were building a new administration building and they were installing one of those central vacuum cleaner machines, where you have the unit in the basement and just plug your hose into wall sockets in each room. Ken knew all about casting, mold-making, patina, all those things. So he duplicated the vacuum wall-sockets—they were bronze plates—and made a whole bunch of them, just exact replicas, except they didn't work. They were dummies. He got in there one night and epoxied his duplicates on, at exactly the perfect height, all over the building.

"This was Ken Cory, to be understated. When he finally picked jewelry, the things he made were magnificent, but it was also his chance to be flamboyant. Because he was casting jacks [from the children's game] and river cobbles, almost anything, instead of precious metals and fine stones. This was his comment on society, but always in miniature and always elegant. You see, this small scale of his is a private world. He was always making these magnificent little things. He was fascinated with copper enameling. Even in high school he was experimenting with making beads. He couldn't figure out how to get the hole in them, so he wrapped fine copper wire [around another wire] to do it. And he wanted, always, everything in his control. He just had a really inquiring mind. He stretched everything he could as far as he could . . . well, in graduate school anyway, but not in high school. In high school he was still very shy and quiet."

Here are, from the start, an obsession with craft and process, rollicking good humor and playfulness, a love for the interesting, quirky or found object, nontraditional techniques—Cory remarked in an early statement, "Every teacher I ever had told me you couldn't cast copper"—and a searing, often bawdy and biting, but always funny, commentary on the repressive mores of 1950s and 60s American society, all rooted in family, day-to-day experiences in the community, the small-town and rural landscapes he grew up in, and the era that shaped him. And all endured throughout his life as essential components in his art.

Double Clutch

California College of Arts and Crafts, Oakland, 1963–1967

"As Ken was finishing up at Pullman High, he had his eye on art school," Beverly Cory remembers. "Robert had in mind a more rigorous intellectual education for us, and insisted on Stanford." But Ken Cory didn't get in, though he was accepted to enter in his second year as a transfer student if his grades were good enough, at least a B average. Instead, he enrolled in WSU that freshman year in 1962, the school just across town from his house, and lived at home. Somehow, during that single year at WSU, he talked Robert into letting him go to art school. In 1963 he left Pullman and entered the B.F.A. program at Oakland's California College of Arts and Crafts, where he would graduate with a degree in Metalsmithing four years later.

The San Francisco Bay Area that Cory moved to in 1963 was a shifting, roiling, social and cultural ground which influenced all aspects of Cory's later life and art, just as those years and all the changes visited by them still vibrate in our culture today. The Beat movement in poetry, theater, and art was in full force. Pop art was emerging. Both in Davis and the Bay Area, California Funk, that elastic crazy quilt of a scene which had grown naturally out of the Beat movement along with Pop and the figurative movement in painting, was exploding, and it shook the foundations of the dominant aesthetics of European and East Coast–based Abstract Expressionism and Modernism. During the years Cory was in the Bay Area, the Vietnam War was escalating, becoming increasingly horrifying. Beat poetry, experimental film, the hippie and antiwar movements, Haight-Ashbury, the People's Park, psychedelic music, and the drug culture were all in the air in the Bay Area, or soon would be. Just think about a small-town kid from rural eastern Washington, driving down the coast in an old Plymouth with soaring fins and tuck-and-roll upholstery to start art school in the giddy heart-of-it-all. Ken Cory was nineteen years old.

Put On, Not Up

Bay Area Art, 1945–1970

The California College of Arts and Crafts, one of the four largest independent art and design schools in the country, was founded in 1907 by Frederick Meyer, a German immigrant and Arts and Crafts movement cabinetmaker.[2] Following the 1906 San Francisco earthquake, which leveled the Mark Hopkins Institute of Art where he had been teaching, Meyer founded the California Guild of Arts and Crafts in Berkeley. His school became the California College of Arts and Crafts when it relocated to the Treadwell Estate in Oakland in 1922. The school has exerted an enormous influence on both the fine arts and crafts throughout its history, but especially in the decades immediately following World War II. Alumni Richard Diebenkorn and Nathan Oliviera helped shape first the Bay Area Abstract Expressionist and later the figurative painting movements in the 1950s. Robert Arneson and Peter Voulkos, also CCAC alumni, helped instigate the ceramics revolution of the 1960s and were at the nerve center of Funk. Faculty members Jack Mendenhall and Mary Snowden and alumnus Robert Bechtle helped found the 1970s Photorealist movement. The list of influential faculty, former students and graduates is long, and includes Dennis Oppenheim, with his influence on conceptual art; John McCracken, in minimalist sculpture; the filmmaker Wayne Wang; Michael McClure, the Beat poet and playwright; and Robin Lasser, David Ireland, Richard Posner, and Manuel Neri, influential artists all.

(Untitled) Hose (pin), 1968
Silver and plastic
1¾ × 2 × 1 in.

Across the Bay from CCAC is the San Francisco Art Institute. In the hills above Oakland, there's the University of California, Berkeley, and down the Bay, Stanford University. Michael McClure, who moved to the Bay Area in 1954, reminds us, "San Francisco was a hotbed of liberalism and Pacific Coastal Rim ideas and environmental consciousness at its early stages, and a place where one could live in a lovely apartment with a view and low rent that an artist might be able to afford."[3] Douglas MacAgy was running the California School of Fine Arts (now the San Francisco Art Institute), the other major independent art school in the Bay Area, in the late 1940s. There, in 1949, MacAgy organized, among many innovations at the school, the Western Round Table on Modern Art, an event that brought to town Marcel Duchamp, who was changing the map of Western art and aesthetics, and Frank Lloyd Wright, one of the century's most daring and influential architects. For his faculty MacAgy hired a powerful group of artists, including Clyfford Still, Hassel Smith, Edward Corbett, Ansel Adams, Mark Rothko, and Ad Reinhardt.

Much has been written about the school's influence on West Coast Abstract Expressionism and that movement's force and presence in northern California during this time, and MacAgy was a powerful figure in this postwar movement. While this influence turned out to be short-lived,[4] as Rebecca Solnit observes, consider these shifts and changes: Clay Spohn, who taught at the California School of Fine Arts, had by 1949 already created his *Museum of Little-Known Objects*, perhaps the first assemblage in the Bay Area, with the help of fellow teachers Richard Diebenkorn, Hassel Smith, and Frank Lobdell. Jay DeFeo, one of

ROBERT ARNESON
Typewriter, 1966
Glazed ceramic
6 x 11½ x 12½ in.
Courtesy of Allan Stone Gallery, New York

the best-known Abstract Expressionists, who painted very little after completing her masterwork, *The Rose,* in 1964, experimented with jewelry-making from the mid-1960s to the early 70s. Clyfford Still, perhaps the most influential painter and teacher in the Bay Area at this time, probably could not have imagined that Burgess Frank Collins, one of his most gifted students, would become the painter Jess, another seminal Funk artist, who met the Beat poet Robert Duncan in 1950 and forged a relationship which endured until Duncan's death in 1988. Elmer Bischoff, David Park and other painters became the Bay Area figurative school. Richard Diebenkorn explored both abstraction and figurative painting. Frank Lobdell was William Wiley's teacher at the San Francisco Art Institute.[5] As a young student, Ken Cory was deeply influenced by Wiley's work and continued to study it carefully throughout his life. The Beat movement brought the writers Robert Duncan, Kenneth Rexroth, Allen Ginsburg, Gary Snyder, Philip Whalen, and Jack Kerouac to the area. By the late 1950s, the migration north from southern California included ceramics artists Peter Voulkos and Robert Arneson as well as Manuel Neri, James Melchert, and David Gilhooly, all deeply involved in the growing Funk movement. Something was happening, and, like MacAgy's tenure at the School of Fine Arts—he was replaced in 1950—mainline Modernism's hold on the most important Bay Area artists would not endure. "For years everything was for the War," the filmmaker James Broughton remembers, "that's why there was this wonderful explosion in 1945 and 1946. Suddenly we knew what we wanted to do. That's when the Bay Area came into flower. Something began to explode for everyone. Wonderful painters. Experimental film began. Wonderful audiences. Everyone was hungry."[6] The sense of release also revealed a hunger for something wholly different from the reigning aesthetics. And as his earliest work shows so clearly, there were few hungrier than the bright, talented Ken Cory, let loose in the fertile, growing metropolis that the Bay Area was becoming in the mid-1960s.

Un-Natural Extension
To thy new mind
If there is such a thing might be about comparison of parallels
and solving problems of expansion. The change from natural
to un-natural if there is such a thing is not always quick and
hidden. You can always watch the solution go down. Like
a ground Hog, Shadows and all. From then on its just a matter
of keeping an eye on the calendar. Wm. T. Wiley 7/3/—

WILLIAM T. WILEY
Un-Natural Extension to Any Man's Mind, 1969
Watercolor and ink on paper, 19 × 24 in.
Courtesy of Wanda Hansen, Sausalito

Throughout his life Ken Cory respected and closely studied William Wiley's work. The similarities between Cory's and Wiley's early lives are remarkable. Consider: Wiley came down the coast to the Bay Area from Richland, Washington—a Columbia Plateau high-desert community that is home to the Hanford Nuclear Reservation, just a hundred miles or so west of Pullman—and studied painting under Frank Lobdell at the San Francisco Art Institute. Wiley went on to teach at the University of California at Davis, along with sculptor Manuel Neri, painters Wayne Thiebaud and Roy De Forest, and ceramicist Robert Arneson. First an Abstract Expressionist painter and widely recognized as one of the most gifted young artists in the Bay Area, he became one of the earliest Funk (or "Phunk," as he wrote it) artists.

In his work Wiley was interested, as Cory would be, in the presence and *resonance* of the object, especially the everyday or found object; in narrative structures and the incorporation of text in his work; and later in sculpture that echoed recognizable objects. If Victor Moore is Cory's first role model as an artist, Wiley is surely his second.

Through the influences of Beat, Funk and Pop, Bay Area art, as well as film, literature, theater, and music, began to radiate irony, wit, delight in visual puns and bawdiness, a spirit of irreverence, absurdity—and revolution. And much of this art explored, reached out for, and irresistibly, *ironically* embraced popular culture—the discarded, the detritus of that American consumer culture which was in a feeding frenzy of prosperity in the postwar years, as the country made its aggressive transition from a wartime to a peacetime economy. The Beat movement was a social phenomenon that by the mid-1950s had spread widely from its centers in San Francisco's North Beach and New York's Greenwich Village. It was a fiercely bohemian youth movement—though including plenty of old leftists, union people, anarchists, and the politically disaffected—full of contradictions, contrasts, and a feeling of deep unease with an increasingly soul-numbing postwar industrial culture desperately trying to ignore the shadow of the bomb. In its beginnings, Beat was an art of the streets and cafes, not the museums and established galleries.

Beat

The lines between Beat and Funk are blurred both aesthetically and temporally. Beat was the postwar, antiestablishment social and cultural phenomenon that encompassed music, film, poetry, and art and was in its highest gear by the mid-1950s. Thomas Albright argues that Funk grew out of Beat, that Funk was a 1960s movement. Beat, he suggests, was more about cultural disaffection, alienation, withdrawal. With their roots in the New York School's myth of the artist as isolated genius, existentialism's recognition of the fragility and alienation of the individual in industrial society, and an instinctive repugnance in response to the sterility of postwar America, the Beats took themselves outside, away even from the fringes of the materialistic, conformist America of the 1950s.

It was a movement that celebrated spontaneity, irreverence, the disaffected, rebellion. It is clear that the Beat movement spawned Funk, that roughly the 1950s are Beat, the 1960s are Funk, and that assemblage, the incorporation of found objects into paintings and sculpture, along with the first spontaneous "happenings," all find their origins in the Beat movement and their fullest expression in Funk. Thomas Albright, who has thoroughly explored this time and its movements, could not decide how to distinguish the two and so settled it this way for us: "Funk or Funk art for the 1960s variety, and funk (instead of funky) for the work that principally reflected the Beat sensibility of the 1950s."[7]

Beat and Funk took hold widely in 1950s and 1960s Bay Area art and spread both north and south on the West Coast. Cory's work would, throughout his life, focus on the object, the image, the everyday *stuff* of American consumer culture, though always in the context of the metalsmithing tradition. Significantly, the art that he saw as a student—by William Wiley, Robert Arneson, Jay DeFeo, Jess, Peter Voulkos, Jim Melchert, Jeremy Anderson, Bruce Conner, and Chicago's Hairy Who, all Beat and Funk people—was an art that was either ambivalent or openly hostile to the art market, to art as something precious and made to "last forever," to both traditional and Modernist aesthetics and rational or intellectual dialogue, an art that celebrated the ordinary, that made the extraordinary *out of* the ordinary. After all, the West Coast is farther away from European traditions, and so those traditions were naturally less important to postwar West Coast artists. Asian, Native American, and above all vernacular culture—cowboys, cars, household objects, the natural world—are the roots for this art. And other influences simmered in this hothouse: the antirational legacy of Dada and Surrealism; a celebration of the absurd as in so much of Funk art; a

Funk

California Funk is difficult to label. As a fundamentally subversive aesthetic, how could it be otherwise? Beat, Funk's precursor, was cool, withdrawn, introspective, whereas Funk was public and often political, part of the social upheavals of the 1960s' antiwar and free speech movements. While closely related to the more theoretical (and theatrical) Dada and Fluxus movements and to Chicago's Hairy Who, Funk was freer, looser, rougher, more spontaneous.

Funk artists reveled in industrial and consumer culture's detritus, in junk and everyday objects. In open and unabashed sexuality and explorations of drug-induced experience. Social and political commentary. A healthy disregard for both aesthetic and material preciousness. A delight in ambiguity, metaphor, language play, improvisation. And assemblage—especially assemblage. Jean Dubuffet coined the term in the early 1950s. Jasper Johns, Robert Rauschenberg, Louise Nevelson, and others were making assemblages in New York at this time, but with a more formal approach. In California, on the other hand . . . Joan Brown remembers: "I guess there was a rebellion basically against the slicker materials. There was a delight taken in using ratty materials. The rattier the better." (Solnit, p. 68)

California Funk was a wide-open, experimental, rebellious aesthetic and social movement with repercussions that we still feel today.

I Ching coin, Tang Dynasty, and (**Untitled**) **Bone, Thumb, Tongue, Pencil** (Pencil Brothers pin), 1986
Pin: champlevé enamel on goldplated copper
1 in. diameter

wildly experimental attitude toward materials; a willingness to mix media and traditions; and the beginnings of assemblage.[8] And then, in contrast with and even in contradiction to Funk's sometimes deeply bitter, ironic celebration of consumer culture, there was also a revival of interest in a whole array of mystical traditions: the Kabala, the Tarot, medieval alchemy, and ancient Chinese and Japanese mystical texts (the *I Ching* would be an enduring influence on Cory's art), which brought with it an emphasis on the magical power of symbols, materials, and objects, on association, metaphor, and narrative. In much of Funk there was an overt spirituality, though a spirituality in stark contrast to the intellectual "purity" of Abstract Expressionism. All these social, cultural, and aesthetic forces

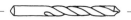

Pop

Pop art has its roots in the revolt against Abstract Expressionism, revolt against, that is, both abstraction and expressionist gestures in the mainstream art of the 1940s and 1950s. Pop was also rooted in the legacy of such rebellious, antirational movements as Dada and Neo-Dada. Pop pretty much came of age for the larger public in the mid-1960s with Roy Lichtenstein's huge, slickly rendered, comic-book-like paintings. Pop art became popular, for, as Thomas Albright says, "People were happy to see painting return to images they found instantly recognizable."

Where artists and critics generally agree is that Pop art simply sought to absorb the banal detritus of consumer culture as a singular, ironic subject. Funk artists sought to bridge the worlds of art and culture, finding art in culture and nature, nature and culture in art. Pop was slick and savvy. Funk, with its roots in the Beat rebellion, was . . . well, funky.

were swirling in the Bay Area art schools, galleries, and studios from the mid-1940s through the 1960s. And from them, Cory began as a Funk artist, carrying the Funk aesthetic and spirit into the Northwest when he joined the Art Department at Central Washington University in 1971.

The history of American metalsmithing and jewelry from the postwar period through the late 1960s has its parallels, though rather loose ones, to the aesthetic upheavals in painting and sculpture in northern California and throughout the country, during the postwar years.[9] Two things first. Unlike modern European crafts, craft work in the United States did not possess a long, established tradition. American jewelers did not have the benefit of an apprenticeship system; they were not trained in the trade, the traditional craft of jewelry-making. There was no orthodoxy, either aesthetic or technical, to inherit or to grow into. Second, there was no single craftsman or movement that served as a fountainhead, a touchstone, for young American jewelers to test themselves against—or to throw over. Some critics argue for the French Art Nouveau jeweler René Lalique (1860–1945) as a kind of "father figure" for modern and contemporary jewelry. Lalique did play an important role in opening the floodgates in jewelry, experimenting with form, techniques, and the use of unusual and surprising materials. But although Lalique was perhaps the single greatest influence on the then-young Art Nouveau movement in jewelry, his influence was mostly limited to that movement and its time.

In another realm, Alexander Calder, Pablo Picasso, André Derain, Max Ernst, and other painters and sculptors occasionally made some jewelry in the decades following World War II, and both European and American metalsmiths saw this work. With the possible exception of Calder's influence on the hammered-silver work of the American metalsmiths Ward Bennett and Harry Bertoia, one cannot confidently trace any direct lineage from these artists' jewelry to American metalsmithing. In the fine arts, Abstract Expressionism—grown out of the European and American political and social upheavals in the decades leading up to and following World War II—was an aesthetic and philosophical debate so basic that painters and sculptors of the 1940s and 50s simply had to confront it. But there was no comparable hegemony in American metalsmithing.[10]

There was a great deal of activity in American metalsmithing in the mid-1940s and throughout the 1950s. The School of American Craftsmen in Rochester, New York, the Cranbrook Academy of Art in Michigan, the California College of Arts and Crafts, the Philadelphia Museum School, and the Boston Museum School all had active and growing metals departments. In Minneapolis, the Walker Art Center mounted the *National Exhibition of Contemporary Jewelry* a number of times from the late 1940s through the 1950s, and in these exhibitions American jewelers had the opportunity to see each other's work and ideas. These shows made clear that Sam Kramer—who was unabashedly using unusual materials such as taxidermist's glass eyes, plastic, and bakelite in his odd, eccentric jewelry—Margaret De Patta, Paul Lobel, Robert Winston, Phil Morton and others were pushing the boundaries for American metalsmiths.

If there *was* a dominant aesthetic in jewelry at midcentury and in the decades following, it was the clean, sleek, highly geometric, often minimalist style which metamorphosed into the Modernist school. Margaret De Patta's work comes out of this aesthetic. And if there is a movement in jewelry that challenges the Modernist, it is the Beat-like, organic, drippy, willfully crude works that were so popular in the late 1950s and throughout the 1960s. George Laisner, one of Cory's teachers at WSU, was making this kind of jewelry in Pullman. But the Beat aesthetic seemed to simply coexist with its Modernist opposite, rather than throwing it over. And then the barriers did begin to dissolve: along with Pop came assemblage, which Sam Kramer was doing earlier, well before Funk. Fred Woell, Robert Ebendorf, Arline Fisch, and others followed Kramer, working in a mix of styles. Their work was a kind of anti-jewelry, rebelling against the Modernist orthodoxy, incorporating found objects, indiscriminately tossing together diverse and random elements, incorporating images and traditions from other cultures, interjecting irreverent humor and political content. This is the work that Ken Cory saw as a young undergraduate and graduate art student.

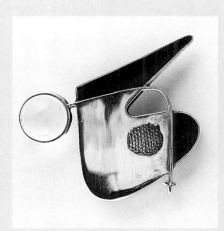

MARGARET DE PATTA
Pin (brooch), 1944
Sterling silver and quartz crystal
2¾ x 2⅜ x ½ in.
Collection of the Oakland Museum of California,
gift of Eugene Bielawski, the Margaret De Patta
Memorial Collection

Margaret De Patta, another artist whose work Cory studied closely as an undergraduate and throughout his life, was one of the most highly respected Modernist metalsmiths. The Oakland Museum of Art has a large collection of her work. Trained as a painter, she became interested in jewelry after she moved to San Francisco in 1929, where she studied metalsmithing with the Armenian craftsman Armin Hairenian.

Though their aesthetics were wildly different, perhaps as much a function of their different generations as anything else, Cory and De Patta shared some remarkably similar attitudes. Here are some observations by Yoshiko Uchida, published in the exhibition catalogue for De Patta's 1976 Oakland Museum exhibition:

"Although she experimented freely, she never lost sight of the function of jewelry, nor of its limitations as to size, weight, durability, and relationship to body structure.

"She was among the first craftsmen to employ new materials of her day . . . 'We should not hesitate to use new material,' she said, 'or to use hitherto unacceptable materials, if they fit within our requirements of good design.'"

Here, De Patta could well be speaking directly to one of the fundamentals underlying Cory's aesthetic and craftsmanship.

"The artistic value of jewelry, she felt, should not be any less than that of sculpture," Uchida observed. And here again we find a remarkable concordance in De Patta's and Cory's beliefs. Both at the beginning of his career and then at the very end of his life, Cory was working at the jeweler's bench making monumental sculpture in miniature.

The sources for Cory's early work were catching fire in the Bay Area right as the 1940s ended, and later in Davis, and in the work of metalsmiths a generation older than he. The repressive, sexually muffled, drab America of the postwar years was beginning to both flower and break apart all at once. Though not the only force for this change, the Bay Area was certainly North America's leading edge. Then too, there were the drugs: bags and bags of pot, peyote, mescaline, and later, LSD. The drug culture was a pivotal influence on many of this generation's artists and their art.[11] Pot and peyote drastically revised the consciousness of many of these artists; with the drugs vision was heightened, the world became infused with possibility. Indeed, *everything* was potential for the bravest and most

imaginative artists in the postwar West Coast art scene. No survey of the highly charged, commentary-driven, sharply satiric, culturally layered art of first the Beat, and then the Funk and Pop movements, can be complete without acknowledging the deep and abiding influence of hallucinogens and pot on this time. Like the effect of the Vietnam War on youth during this period, and like the breaking down of the repressive sexual mores of the 1940s and 50s, the drug culture of the 1960s and 70s tattooed the era, and its art, in ways we cannot ignore. Ken Cory came of age in a rebellious, revolutionary time. His vision, his imaginative gifts, his themes, were forged as much in the creative cacophony of the San Francisco Bay Area of the 1960s as in the small Palouse Hills town where he grew up.

J. FRED WOELL
Jet Lag (pin), 1988
Cast silver and moonstone
2 × 2½ × ½ in.
Collection of the artist

The Spirit of Making
CCAC, 1964–1967

Cory had made some jewelry during his freshman year at WSU. Quite by chance—art history is full of these moments—he had wandered by a workshop where students were fabricating jewelry. "Before that," he said, "I thought jewelry came out of factories and it was something you needed big machines to make. So I took a jewelry class and all of a sudden, it was like magic. I was making things out of metal with just a few simple hand tools. And I thought, 'Boy here is a whole area that hasn't been explored yet.'"[12] The workshop was led by George Laisner, an

Portrait of George A. Laisner,
ca. mid-1960s

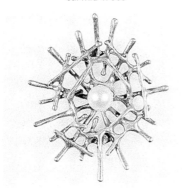

GEORGE A. LAISNER
Brooch, ca. early 1960s
Sterling silver and pearl
2 x 2 x ½ in. approx.

émigré from Czechoslovakia who had studied at the Art Institute of Chicago and the University of Chicago, and had been teaching at WSU since 1937. His work, in sculpture and jewelry, was an early influence. As is common for most artists, Cory's first works are fully imitative—in this case, of the work of George Laisner and Margaret De Patta. Though he would move far, far away from Laisner's and De Patta's aesthetic, openly rebelling against Laisner, especially, as a graduate student, Cory always acknowledged his debt to these two artists.

Ceramics were in the ascendant at CCAC when Cory arrived to study there. In the Bay Area generally, and soon nationally, there was a full-blown revolution going on in the ceramics community, led by Arneson, Voulkos, and their followers. The CCAC metals department that Cory entered was not as dynamic as the ceramics area. But by the mid-1960s, all that was changing for metalsmithing—and glass, wood, and fiber as well. The ground had been broken in the earlier work of Kramer, Woell, Ebendorf, and soon thereafter in the Northwest by Ramona Solberg, Don Tompkins, and others, all those pioneers who veered away from the mainstream. The change became even more dramatic when Cory's earliest work—*Tongue, Reflector,* and *Wave* (all from 1967), *Pin, Set of Five,* and *Zipper* (all 1968), made in the last days at CCAC and when he was a graduate student at WSU—was widely exhibited, reproduced in journals and catalogues, and toured, along with other new work of this time. This is the first of Cory's work seen by young metalsmiths of his own generation: Elliot Pujol, Lane Coulter, Gary Noffke, Lynda Watson-Abbott (then Lynda Watson), Jan Brooks, Mary Hu, and others. Together, this generation of metalsmiths remapped the American art jewelry and metalsmithing landscapes.

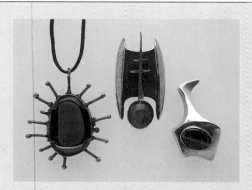

These early *Fish* and *Form* pins strongly evoke the reigning Modernist aesthetic, in jewelry, of the midcentury years. Modernism was also the leading aesthetic in CCAC's metals department when Cory arrived there: clean-lined, minimalist, highly stylized abstracted forms—what Cory called "Mo Derne," and Lane Coulter and others "Scando-Mod," after the popular sleek, light Scandinavian design in furniture which had such an enormous influence throughout the crafts in the postwar era.

Early untitled student work: **Snot Pendant**, ca. 1962 and two pins, **Fish** and **Form**, ca. 1964–65 Left to right: brass and beach rock, 2½ × 2 × ½ in.; silver and agate, 2¼ × 1 ⅛ × ½ in.; silver and tiger eye, 1 × 2 × ½ in.

The pendant, perhaps done while Cory was studying with George Laisner—it looks a great deal like much of Laisner's work—was made during Cory's freshman year at Pullman, and is typical of the contemporary aesthetic that overlapped and then temporarily replaced the Modernist style as all the old aesthetic canons began breaking down on the East and West Coasts in the early 1950s. It is what Cory called "snot jewelry." Distinct from the Modernist look, snot jewelry is beatnik-like, crude, heavy-handedly organic. Nancy Worden says, "Almost everybody who made jewelry in the late 1950s, 60s and early 70s went through a phase of one or both of these styles."

Not long after he arrived at CCAC, Cory met Ruth Tamura, now the Deputy Director of Hawaii's Plantation Village at Waipahu Cultural Garden Park in Hawaii. Both started at CCAC that same year and lived in the dorm, he on the first floor and she on the second floor in a room above Cory. They soon became a couple. He took Tamura home with him that first Christmas break. They were close all four years they were at CCAC. She remembers his car, a turquoise Plymouth sedan with fins and a great tuck-and-roll leather interior. She also remembers, "Ken never liked big cities or densely populated areas. I did think he was one of the better-traveled people I knew at CCAC. He had been to Africa, Central and South America, Mexico [all those summer trips organized by Robert Cory]. And though I would often ask if he would like to return to some of those locations, he had no interest in repeating a trip.

"During those years," Tamura remembers, "if Ken wasn't in class, the studio at school or in his home work space, if he wasn't working in his sketchbook drawing, if we weren't going to galleries and exhibitions, we were going to Chinatown

Interested in ceramics from an early age, Cory made a small group of odd and engaging pots while a CCAC student. They show his natural, early understanding of the emerging Funk aesthetic and the ferociously unique vision he brought to his art. By screwing that plastic reflector onto the flattened side of one pot, and by affixing a common hardware store spigot on the mouth of another, we see him experimenting, very early on, with an unusual collision of materials, and his openness to objects of material culture. We also see how effortlessly funny he was.

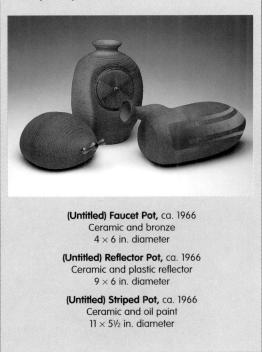

(Untitled) Faucet Pot, ca. 1966
Ceramic and bronze
4 × 6 in. diameter

(Untitled) Reflector Pot, ca. 1966
Ceramic and plastic reflector
9 × 6 in. diameter

(Untitled) Striped Pot, ca. 1966
Ceramic and oil paint
11 × 5½ in. diameter

or junking at scrap yards, the seaside, or railroad tracks. We would go to San Francisco's Chinatown a lot. Often enough so that we knew which day was garbage day. We would make our visits to Chinatown the night before to collect as many wooden boxes as we could. Sometimes we would even find large covered tin containers stacked on the sidewalks waiting to be picked up by the trash men. Ken used these boxes and tin cans to create a box wall that became his bookcase for found objects, books, rocks, bottles—anything that he had found and thought looked special." Throughout the rest of his life, Cory's living spaces were filled with boxes, shelves, bookcases, from floor to ceiling, covering walls—and all filled with his hundreds of tiny objects and various artifacts of his extraordinary, diverse collections. He simply loved small, beautiful, common, and unusual quirky stuff.

Teachers at CCAC encouraged and often required students to visit exhibitions in the Bay Area museums, galleries, and art centers. "Ken and I would often make trips to the de Young Museum, the Asian Art Museum, the San Francisco Art Institute, the Legion of Honor, and the many private galleries," Tamura recalls. "Some of the artists whose work we would encounter included Jim Melchert, Jeremy Anderson, William Wiley, Peter Volkous, Robert Arneson, and Richard Shaw. We both took

English classes from Michael McClure, the Beat poet. We attended a number of poetry readings and happenings featuring McClure and Ginsberg. I remember Ken took a class in filmmaking, I think from Bruce Conner, and he made an 8 mm film on fire using the Bill Haley song, 'Great Balls of Fire' as the sound track. Besides the Beat people and the West Coast scene, Ken liked the imagery and aesthetic of the Hairy Who."

At CCAC, Cory learned electroforming, enameling, and casting. He studied drawing with Ralph Boyd Borge, and he had Marty Streich and Byron Wilson for metalsmithing and jewelry. From the very start, though he did use silver and gold, he used copper, other everyday materials, and odd found objects in his jewelry. He would often experiment with silver casting around found objects, trying to find ways to capture the surprising. "I think it would be correct to say that he was among the group of emerging jewelers who were dismissing the recognized metals, gold and silver, for other metals and plastics. Victor Moore was probably the most important influence on Ken though," Tamura observes. "I remember meeting Mr. Moore within twenty-four hours after having arrived in Pullman that first Christmas break. Victor Moore I am sure nurtured much of Ken's interest in collecting, in how he viewed found objects, in fostering his recycling instincts, in

(Untitled) Red Reflector (pin), 1967
Cast copper and plastic reflector
1½ x 2 x ½ in.

Ken's questioning and rethinking media usage—much of his artistic spirit and media innovation were probably because of his mentor and teacher. Ken always had enormous respect for Mr. Moore."

Following graduation, Cory left CCAC and went home again, beginning his graduate studies at WSU. He did return for one year to teach at CCAC after completing his graduate work at Pullman—Tamura was also teaching at CCAC at that time. Tamura remembers, "He never liked using the telephone and would only write an occasional letter. When he returned, he expected everything to be the same. But he had changed and so had I." During his year at CCAC he lived in the family cabin on Mad Creek—the "Mad House" family and friends still call it —high in the Coast Range more than three hours away from Oakland and CCAC. He grew distant from Tamura.

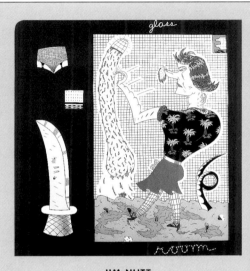

JIM NUTT
Running Wild, 1969
Acrylic on wood and Plexiglas
46 × 43½ in.
Courtesy of Phyllis Kind Gallery, Chicago–New York

The Hairy Who

The Hairy Who was a group of six Chicago artists—Jim Nutt, Gladys Nilsson, James Falconer, Suellen Rocca, Karl Wirsum and Art Green—who had all met as students at the School of the Art Institute of Chicago in the early 1960s. Though only in existence for four years, between 1966 and 1969, and mounting just five exhibitions—in 1966, 1967, and 1968 at the Hyde Park Art Center in Chicago, a 1968 show at the Gallery of the San Francisco Art Institute (which Ken Cory saw) as Nutt and Nilsson both taught at Sacramento State in the late 1960s, and a final exhibition in 1969 at the Corcoran Gallery of Art in Washington, D.C.— the Hairy Who was nonetheless enor- mously influential in creating the Chicago-based imagist school. The Hairy Who artists had many similar interests, in- cluding in their paintings and constructions popular kitsch, comic book imagery, toys, punning language play, and an interest in outsider art as both a source for their own art and as serious art in and of itself. Contemporary with the group but not formally part of the Hairy Who, the Chicago imagist painters Ed Paschke and Roger Brown shared much of the Hairy Who's spirit and approach.

As Ruth Tamura mentions, Ken Cory admired the art interests, artistic style, and the aesthetic spirit of this group. He liked their rebelliousness too. The Hairy Who work dis- played in the Bay Area was one of the major influences in Ken Cory's work and aesthetic style, visible especially in the sinuous, twisted, coiling, meandering forms emerging from the basic geometric shapes of his early works.

Compass

Washington State University, 1967–1969

Oddly and significantly for this story, there were no jewelry or metalsmithing programs at WSU at the time Cory started graduate school there. "I wanted to be left alone to develop on my own," Cory said. "It was a perfect two years. There were other people to talk to, but they let me go in the direction I wanted."[13] Yes, there *were* other people to talk to: the faculty included George Laisner, painter Gaylen Hansen, and art historian Arthur Okazaki, all serious artists and good teachers. Their students included Cory; Les LePere; Victor Moore; sculptor Jack Dollhausen, and painter Robert Helm (Dollhausen and Helm both returned to teach at WSU); Ed Gnaedinger, the former mayor of Palouse, Washington, who though no longer an active artist is engaged in community and governmental affairs in the Pullman area; and the conceptual artist Iain Baxter, now living in Windsor, Canada, who founded the N. E. Thing Company in the late 1960s. A parodic, satirical, conceptual art "corporation," the company took as its mission shaking up the status quo in the

ROBERT HELM
Falling Hour, 1986
Mixed media on wood
19⁵⁄₁₆ × 26 in.
Neuberger Museum of Art, Purchase College, State University of New York; museum purchase with funds made available from the Awards in the Visual Arts Program with assistance from the Roy R. Neuberger Endowment Fund

art world and bringing art out of the galleries directly into people's lives.

It was a powerful group of students, teachers, and friends.

No Ideas but in Things

The First Jewelry, 1967–1971

During this time, Cory continued the experimentation with metal and jewelry he'd begun at CCAC, inventing a technique of his own for casting copper and silver. Instead of making a traditional wax model, he carved or constructed balsa-wood forms, covered these with a plaster-like investment, and then burned out the wood, leaving the impression of the grain behind. The surface texture of the cast-copper pins evoked eastern Washington's dry, weathered wood fences, barns, and other farm outbuildings he'd been looking at all his life. "I was interested in the relationship between man-made things and decay," he says. "It came from looking at all those wonderful old barns and thinking about minimalist art—when I saw the different shapes of the roofs. But the barns didn't have the slickness of minimalist art. They were falling over."[14] Lane Coulter, now teaching at the Institute of American Indian Art in Santa Fe, suspects that this technique grew out of Cory's isolation. "At first he didn't know any better," Coulter says. "He didn't know that you used wax to make a mold, so he used what he was familiar with. He'd made all those model cars and carved balsa as a kid, so these were materials he knew, materials that he was intimate with. You have to remember that to some degree Ken was pretty isolated in the middle of Washington State, the desert there. And in his jewelry he took full advantage of everything that was around him."

There are a number of pieces from this time—*Tongue* and *Wave* (1967); *Pin, Set of Five, Zipper, Hose,* and *Red Snake* (all 1968); *Shift* and *Levers* (1970); and *Rope* (1971)—that strongly embody Cory's basic conceptual and aesthetic concerns,

Tongue (pin), 1967
Silver, amber, and leather
2 × 1½ × ½ in.

right at the beginning. Virtually *all* his work from these years generated excitement in the crafts community.

Tongue is cast silver, with a small amber stone set onto its right edge, and a piece of leather. It is both very feminine—a soft, bulging shape rises from the left edge and extends out over the leather tongue itself; the stone is so much like a nipple—and simultaneously masculine in its overall squarish, badge-like shape. And of course, there is the bawdy character of the leather tongue. This piece encompasses many aspects of the young artist's conceptual interests: jewelry-making itself, that is, the tradition; a wrestling with very small scale; organic form, especially shapes based on the eastern Washington Palouse country he grew up in; the use of unexpected and surprising materials; and his enduring, subtle sense of humor. In *Tongue* he created a traditional piece of jewelry, a small exquisite object meant to be worn on the body as decoration. The imaginative depth and surprising power in this pin are entirely his own vision. Drawing on the craft of tuck-and-roll upholstery he'd learned in making over his Plymouth, he took that

piece of leather, fabricated it in the tuck-and-roll method, and has it languidly hanging out at the viewer. *Tongue*, like so many of these earliest pieces (and later ones), is funny, irreverent, inventive, and daring.

Set of Five (1968) was reproduced in the July 21, 1969, issue of *Newsweek* in the article "Crafting Their Own World," which covered new directions in the crafts revival of the late 1960s. The article opens

(Untitled) Set of Five (pins), 1968
Cast copper, brass, and plastic
1¼ × 1¼ × ¾ in. each

with the sentence, "Out of the ashes of a technological society that virtually obliterated him, the American craftsman, like the phoenix, has risen anew."[15] Cory must have loved that line. Like *Drain* (1968), *Shift* (1969), and *Levers* and *Shell* (both 1970), which share a great deal conceptually and imagistically with it, *Set of Five* is emblematic of Cory's enduring conceptual interests in the presence of machinery (and especially its potential to be beautiful), the image of the pyramid, and the mystical traditions associated with the number 5. In the center of each of the five copper pyramidal forms—and they are tiny, each only a little over an inch on a side—is set an exquisitely craft-

(Untitled) Shift (pin), 1969
Cast copper, brass, and ivory
1¾ × 1½ × ½ in.

ed brass and red plastic gearshift lever. On the right side and cast as part of each pyramid are the raised numerals 1 through 5. Cory loved machines and worked with them all his life. The pyramid Les LePere refers to as their "mother image." And the number 5, which he likely learned about primarily from the *I Ching* as an undergraduate, was a deeply personal compositional tool that Cory returned to again and again. The presence of the number 5 is examined in depth in the discussion of his second body of work.

And then there is sex. *Red Snake*, *Zipper*, and *Pin* (all 1968), as well as *Drain* and *Hose* (1968), and *Sword* (1970), share this theme, a sexual resonance and playful-

(Untitled) Drain (pin), 1968
Bronze, Plexiglas, and found object
2 × 1¼ × 1 in.

ness. Bright orange/red, bulging, curving, thrusting Plexiglas and plastic appendages are attached to the cast-copper and silver surfaces—softened, flowing, bulging shapes he brought to the work from the natural world. The images are both fundamentally organic—bullwhip kelp, shoot, root, tendril, vine, stamen—and plainly erotic—penis, tongue, finger. *Zipper* is simply direct, technically and conceptually stunning in its bringing together cast silver, brass, and that touch of leather—skin—where the zipper hangs open. In these pieces he is playing with oppositions: decay and regeneration, organic and man-made, plant and machine, hard metal and soft plastic, the

(Untitled) Zipper (pin), 1963
Silver, brass, and leather
2 × 1½ × ½ in.

roughened and weathered surfaces of cast copper and the slickness of the plastic. These works, as *images*, are bold, surprising, and unique for their time. The use of unusual materials—cast copper, Plexiglas, plastic, leather—all those references to machinery and machine parts, plus the openly bawdy, sexual images, was startling. In 1976, the English curator Ralph Turner observed, "Cory explores whatever materials he uses to the full. His ideas are fresh, explicit and consistent."[16]

Cory's work, from the earliest to the last, was *essentially* based on the forms he found around him: stones, appliances, trailers—lots of those in eastern Washington—old farm buildings, organic forms like shells (he'd brought them along from summer trips), women's breasts and hips, tendrils, roots, branches, stems, streams, the snake and stream-like shapes that railroad beds and roads make on the vastly open intermountain Western landscape. Throughout his lifetime, his image vocabulary was highly personal and continually deepening. The objects, the images he incorporated into his work were specific, concrete, an expanding visual language of signs, metaphors, and personal references. He was at the beginning of what would be a lifelong exploration of the *meaning* of objects in his life, in our lives. And unlike most of his peers in Funk, Cory never used images randomly. There is an intentionality in all this early work. The objects he found himself drawn to were dense with potential. From the beginning, he was making *jewelry as sculpture*, work resonating with decorative and technical tradition, yet saturated with his own imaginative and intellectual vision.

This first body of work gained immediate notice among metalsmiths and curators. By the time he had completed graduate school, or very soon thereafter, he had been featured in the 1969 *Newsweek* article on the crafts revival—though with a hopelessly

(Untitled) Wave (pin), 1967
Cast copper and cast resin
1½ × 2 × ½ in.

Ken Cory, ca. 1968

poor photograph of his piece. The *Newsweek* article mentions the 1970 Smithsonian Institution's *Objects: USA*[17] exhibition and catalogue organized by curator Lee Nordness and Paul Smith, Director of the Museum of Contemporary Crafts in New York, which also included Cory, one of fewer than a dozen artists his age in that encyclopedic exhibition. S. C. Johnson & Son, Inc., the makers of Johnson Wax, long a major corporate collector of crafts, funded the exhibition and tour, and purchased one of Cory's works, now in the collection of the American Craft Museum. In 1968 his work was included in New York's Museum of Contemporary Crafts' *Objects Are . . .* exhibition, the next year in their *Young Americans 1969* exhibition, and in 1970 he had a major one-man exhibition there. In the following decade his work was regularly included in shows across North America and in Japan: Pasadena, Oakland, Toronto, Boulder, Richmond, Brockport, Atlanta, Sacramento, Pittsburgh, Tokyo, Kyoto, in dozens of curated exhibitions and in college galleries. Working entirely on his own, he had produced a remarkably mature, influential body of work. The photograph of Cory in *Objects USA*—craftspeople always call this catalogue the "Johnson Wax" book—shows a bearded, long-haired, slightly smiling young man in a fringed leather jacket sitting comfortably behind the wheel of a convertible looking over his right shoulder directly at us. He is right at home. He is famous.

The Boys

The Pencil Brothers

Ken Cory met Les LePere back in the summer of 1966 in a summer ceramics class at WSU. LePere was driving his father's 1949 school-bus-yellow Ford pickup that night, a truck that Cory loved on sight. After class, Cory bummed a ride home from LePere. This is how LePere remembers that night: "On the way home we stopped in an alley in down-

58

town Pullman and scavenged the trash bins. That evening we found some toy soldiers—we had both played with them as kids—and some reflectors. That very first set of experiences set the tone and philosophy of our friendship that carried over into all the art we later made together. To try to make something unusual, to use common everyday happenings as the research method for formulating handmade art, and to use the art as the direction for research. Reflections from one's everyday observations. We were naughty along the way. We balked against the establishment of Abstract Expressionism because of the narrowness of it visually and the idea that in order for art to be good it had to be big. What!!! During these first shared adventures we performed countless conceptual-like acts—it was big in California—and had fun tricking, deceiving, and making humor with people, things, and subjects."

Out of an admired truck—both Cory and LePere loved American car culture, one thing you do in the West is *drive*—a mutual love of junk and the found object, childhood toys and similar ribald, punning, and unaffected good humors, a friendship was made. LePere is an artist, graphic designer, and wheat farmer living in rural eastern Washington—you may have seen his book cover for the Tom Robbins novel *Still Life with Woodpecker*. He and Cory shared far more, though, than cars, toys, and dirty jokes. As young art school graduate students, both recognized, or sensed may be more accurate here, the

PENCIL BROTHERS
Pop Quiz (wall piece), 1973
Enamel on copper, glass, and found objects
6¾ × 4¼ × ¾ in.
Collection of Leslie LePere

increasing bankruptcy of the New York–based Modernist aesthetic, a bankruptcy perhaps felt with special intensity by small-town, intermountain Westerners. Both loved the irreverent, and knew how powerful it could be as satire and social commentary. Both loved the rolling Palouse country, the Columbia Plateau's channeled scablands, the vernacular architecture of farm buildings, the presence of monolithic grain elevators on the landscape, the dusty dirt roads. Eastern Washington's Palouse Hills country *is* the Palouse because the volcanoes of the Cascade Range have been spewing their ash off and on for tens of thousands of years and it's been piling up in eastern Washington, drifting and forming the dramatic, and enormously fertile, rolling topography. And like the land, they both loved the cars and trucks they drove around those hills. LePere remembers Cory saying one night, "You shouldn't make any art that you can't carry in your car." LePere knew exactly what he was talking about.

"Ken and I spent over a year together in graduate school in Pullman," LePere says. "This gave us ample time to sharpen our skills of junking, picnicking on the river, and turning the things we saw and photographed into points of departure for our art. We put our ideas, gathered mostly out of nature, in sketchbooks, often laughing at the weird, funky, special, odd things we saw and loved. Most of the stuff we liked was not made by other artists! The ultimate, for us,

On the Washington State University campus, near the west side of Bryan Hall, is an unusual drinking fountain, its square concrete base capped with a brick-patterned pyramid. A single narrow-gauge iron railroad track pierces the body of the thing, disappearing in one side and thrusting abruptly out the other. It was commissioned as a gift for the school by Sigma Tau, the engineering fraternity. Growing up, Ken Cory saw this structure hundreds of times. Remember, the Cory family walked everywhere in town. Les LePere and Cory called this the "mother image," and their fascination with it led them, and led Cory in his individual work, to incorporate it into many pieces over the years, among them *Set of Five, Wave, Red Snake, Pin,* and one of Ken Cory's last pins, *Fire.* Les LePere says, "It set us off; it was unusual and strange and humorous. It was beautiful, quiet, and powerful."

Artist unknown
Sigma Tau drinking fountain ("mother image")
Cast concrete
48 × 20 × 20 in. approx.
Bryan Hall, Washington State University, Pullman

was spending a weekend making Ken's thesis show out of flour, salt, and water. Miniature sculpture, pins they were. You see, each graduate student was expected to give a piece from his thesis show to the school's permanent collection as a gift. But Ken did not want to give one of his copper pieces to them. So he and I and a couple of girls we knew made a whole show of Cory-like flour-and-water shapes, painted them, glued on some pin-backs, and that's what he turned in for his thesis show. Naturally the school decided it didn't want one of those pieces.

"Making a thing precious from an utterly common material, that was the real thing to us. It jacked us to find that we shared so many ideas that could be applied to our joy in discovery and making things. Juxtaposition of opposites to create balance. We drank beer and chased girls. We were mystified by our peers, who liked us but thought our use of recognizable objects in our art was confused. Didn't stop us! And you know, ironically, in 1970 the school paid $300 for one of his copper pins for their collection."

During the year that Cory returned to teach at CCAC, 1970–71, there was one development in his work that would have enormous impact over the next decade. LePere says, "I was working on my thesis in 1970 at WSU and it encompassed everyday objects as the subject. Ken was at CCAC in Oakland, so we began working on individual ideas and components of works and when we got together

we combined the parts, and sometimes we mailed parts back and forth to each other. When we finished something, we signed the thing 'Art Team.'" This is the beginnings of the Pencil Brothers, Cory's and LePere's nearly decade-long partnership, a little-known—outside metalsmithing—art collaboration. There is much history to tell here before looking more closely at the works from this period.

Back in graduate school, Cory and LePere had collaborated on one piece, *Homage to Bob Helm* (1969), which they mounted as a two-man,

PENCIL BROTHERS
Homage to Bob Helm (pin), 1969
Cast copper, brass, silver, wood, Plexiglas,
drawing, photo, and silk
1¾ × 2 × ½ in
Collection of Leslie LePere

one-piece exhibition. Bob Helm was then a graduate school peer of theirs. Largely to tweak the faculty and the reigning aesthetic of the day, Cory and LePere wanted to work in opposition to the idea so dominant in art school classrooms and studios of their time, that to be important art had to be big—LePere's voice here: "What!!!"—that art should occupy large space and make dramatic, even if minimally dramatic, gestures. So LePere embellished an aerial photograph of the Pullman campus, including Bryan Hall where the "mother image" fountain is, and Cory cast a tiny copper frame for the piece. It is quietly, oddly beautiful and funny as a send-up of the formal idea of an art exhibit. They made some more things together, mailing work back and forth and signing them "Art Team," and by 1972 they began to spend increasingly more time working together.

In the Heart
Ellensburg, 1972

In 1972 Cory left California and the Mad House and moved to Ellensburg to begin teaching at Central Washington State College, taking Don Tompkins' position. That year Art Team, the initial Cory-LePere art partnership, became the Pencil Brothers. And he met Merrily Tompkins and Nancy Worden, who, along with LePere, were his three closest lifelong friends.

Don Tompkins, an early Pop jeweler, taught metalsmithing and jewelry in the art department at Central Washington State College in Ellensburg for fourteen years, overlapping with Ramona Solberg, who taught there from 1956 to 1967. Born in Everett, Washington, and a graduate of the University of Washington, Tompkins was married to a native Philadelphian who loathed the rural isolation and harsh climate of central Washington's high desert country. In 1971 Tompkins took a position with New York University and left Washington State. Ken Cory was hired to replace him. Tompkins' jewelry—a rich, narrative-based, and funny conglomeration of popular cultural, political, and social commentary—was likely not a direct influence on Cory's work.[18] Cory already had his own beliefs and a maturing aesthetic. But Tompkins' work was surely a powerful legitimizing force

DON TOMPKINS
Banting and Best (pendant), 1971
Sterling silver and found objects
3 × 5 × ½ in.
Collection of Merrily Tompkins

and experience for Cory at this time. In Tompkins' jewelry there are a number of elements that Cory was also using in his own work, or would be soon: the story; objects of consumer culture; low cultural references like the comics, TV, cartoons, games; and biting social satire. But in Tompkins' jewelry there is a rougher, more overtly narrative and political gesture and manner. Tompkins was a tableau-maker, a set designer in miniature, a cartoonist in metal. In his jewelry Cory was, always, sly and subtle, circumspect, rigorously punning, careful and attentive to traditions and craft.

Following graduate school, Les LePere had moved to Seattle, married, and was part of the embryonic art community just developing in that still relatively unsophisticated city on Puget Sound. In the early 1970s, there were very few galleries in Seattle and virtually no active, cohesive art community. San Francisco was the center of the West Coast's art scene. But down on Yesler Way in the heart of Seattle's Pioneer Square, there was a small hole-in-the-wall called Manolides Gallery, run by Jimmy Manolides. At the Manolides Gallery, and at the then-new art space called "and/or," founded by Anne Focke, still an arts activist in the Northwest today, much of the best Bay Area work was being exhibited. Seattle artists were also beginning to show their own new work in these two galleries, including Les LePere and a young artist named Merrily Tompkins—Don Tompkins' kid sister. Naturally, LePere and Merrily Tompkins met, sometime in 1972. And just

RAMONA SOLBERG
Button Rule (pendant), 1980
Bronze, brass, and found objects
4 × 3¼ × ¼ in.
Collection of Marion Gartler

MERRILY TOMPKINS
Snatch Purse, 1975
Sterling silver, champlevé enamel on copper, cowhide,
beaver fur, velvet, and ermine tails
5 × 4 × 3 in.
Collection of the artist

as naturally, Merrily Tompkins met Les LePere's best friend, Ken Cory.

Cory and Merrily Tompkins would soon become lovers. Tompkins traveled by train from Seattle to Ellensburg to visit him, or they saw each other on Cory's trips to Seattle. They remained the closest of friends until he died; she saw him in Ellensburg just two days before his death. "I remember him being very handsome and mysterious, driving a ragtop MG and wearing a headband. Whatever he said, I could tell it was only the tip of the iceberg of what he was thinking. I was dying to get in there and hear the rest. When I finally did, it was just wonderful, because guess what: I knew what he was talking about. And in a way, he kind of introduced me to myself. He could be like a cheerful, excited, inquisitive kid in those times . . . the best, funniest pal you could hope for. Smart as a whip and goofy all at once. Perfectly willing to stick his neck out and learn something or just have fun, not necessarily in that order.

"He taught me to trust my instincts and my own vision, as an artist and a person," Tompkins says. "One of the best things about Ken was the way he could make things so down to earth, even the most abstract, ethereal idea or observation, he could hook that concept to something just so humorous and logical and personal. That's part of why he was such a good teacher. I can see him sitting by the river, throwing rocks in—after he looked at them and handled them plenty—frowning and puzzling over one thing or another: how to make enamel from ground-up beer bottles, composing the most ridiculously finely crafted double-entendre lyrics to a country and western song, figuring out how to fix a clutch with a fat lady's bra. He had an awesomely broad (and I'm sure he would have made full use of that pun!) base of knowledge and simply delighted in problem-solving."

Tompkins lived in Gleed, Washington, a tiny town west of Yakima on the way toward Naches and White Pass, and taught art in Yakima for a few years in the mid-1970s. She and Cory cruised junk stores and flea markets together, camped in the Yakima River Canyon at Umptatum or on the Columbia, took road trips in her VW Beetle or his MG to Zillah to eat at El Ranchito, cruised the bone-jarring dirt roads high in the Manastash hills, explored up into the Cascades, floated all day on rafts on the Columbia near Vantage. In the years that Tompkins and Ken Cory were together, they also went to the Summervail Conference in Colorado several times.

> One time we were naked by a river and having trouble getting comfortable lying on the rocks. Ken said it was an example of poor figure-ground relationship.
> —Merrily Tompkins

After she decided to return to Seattle, and did, she was surprised to get a letter from Cory proposing marriage. "I guess I shouldn't have been surprised," Tompkins says. "I knew he cared for me, and at that point in his life it would have been like pulling his own teeth for him to actually say the damn words. Besides, I never felt the need to force them out of him—his teeth or the words. A proposal— it went like this: 'I think we should get married. I don't think you should move to Seattle. I love you.'—was probably less scary for him than saying much about how he felt. We were playmates first and foremost. I don't think he liked the idea of me not being around to play with, and that forced him to spill his beans."

She remembers, "Ken simply liked beautiful things. There wasn't an ugly thing in his house. He wouldn't get a washer and dryer because he didn't like the way they looked. And why small? He just liked being able to fit all his work into a suitcase under his bed. Treasures, I think. And I think he made jewelry instead of bigger-scale art for several reasons: First of all, he loved that scale. Think of all those little things in those bottle crates and in every nook and cranny of his house. Another factor was his affection for, as he called them, the 'noble metals.' He liked to work with silver and gold. And jewelry is nice because it feels good too. You can take it around with you. I also know that Ken loved to go into uncharted territory and hardly anyone else was making jewelry with intellectual content . . . I mean using jewelry as a means of expressing an idea. Mostly people were just producing body decoration, shapes and designs, a lot of cast abstract stuff. During this time there was a lot of beautifully crafted jewelry, but nothing with any thought-provoking, storytelling stuff in it. My brother Don and Ken shared a delight in being challenged creatively. Maybe Ken learned that from Robert. Maybe figuring out how to make his own kind of jewelry sprang from the same inventive, devilish spot in Ken that made him decide to transplant my sunroof with a jury-rigged hacksaw. It was like a dare.

> Merrily Tompkins had bought a '65 VW Beetle to replace one she'd wrecked on black ice in the Yakima River Canyon. The wrecked one had a sunroof, which she loved, but the new one didn't. As she tells it, "Ken went to work doing a transplant. With a hacksaw, he cut the sunroof out of the wreck and a corresponding hole in the new car, and made a gasket out of an inner tube, and sealed it all in with Indian Head and bolted her on. It never leaked. The only hitch was that he broke the sawblade on a Sunday in the middle of the job and the only hardware store in Ellensburg was closed. So he made a handle from an elbow-shaped tree branch and bolted the broken blade in there and finished the job that way. It took about ten hours. We went to San Francisco together in that car."

"Ken's work is just immaculately crafted and he loved that part of it . . . making a beautiful hinge or clasp, impeccably set stones, flawless solder joints. Add that to the idea, the content, and you got yourself some real entertainment. On top of that, you get to strap the thing on and walk around with it. What could be better?"

Theirs was a long relationship. Together they were daring and funny, spontaneous and cheerfully reckless, and cared little for appearances, surfaces, social expectations, rules. Tompkins was never in any sense Cory's student. Throughout their long friendship, they made work side-by-side, but independently as peers, sharing ideas and professional gossip, helping and supporting each other. Then, not long after Tompkins moved to Seattle, a young woman whom he had known previously only as a student would become his next important romantic and artistic partner.

Sometime in the early summer of 1972, Nancy Worden, at the time a seventeen-year-old Ellensburg High School senior, walked over to Ken Cory's house, knocked on the door and asked him if she could take his beginning jewelry class the next quarter. Nancy Worden's mother and stepfather were professors on the CWU faculty in Education and English. Worden was bored in school, as so many gifted students are. She wanted to learn metalsmithing. Cory told her all right, if she bought her own tools. "I figured that he just said that to run me off," Worden

NANCY WORDEN
Initiation Necklace, 1977
Silver, copper, rhodonite, and found objects
28 × 3 × ½ in.
Collection of the artist

says, "but I bought all the tools he told me to and took the class." And she was good. She worked with Cory during her senior year in high school and the next year enrolled at CWU. She studied with him for a full six years, including one year of graduate study, until leaving to finish her graduate work with Gary Noffke at the University of Georgia in Athens. Sometime late in those six years she and Cory became lovers, eventually living together in Cory's house.

Worden says, "He was a man who was self-contained in so many ways. He liked to know that he could do everything for himself—cook, sew, any kind of home repairs, car repairs. What was missing in his life, though, was a family—his own family. And he gave me so much, especially the license to be myself and to be different from other people. He made me feel funny, pretty, and smart. And we did so many things together, road trips, sitting and walking by the river, cruising junk stores, playing cards, cooking together. We shared a fascination with jewelry and technique and history, art history, but not like they teach it in school.

"I was his academic protégé and sounding board, emotional confidant, and later, a peer. I feel lucky that I was one of Ken's students. What he created for us was an atmosphere completely lacking in pretense or convention. We didn't have to break any rules, he had already done that. I knew a lot about academic politics from my folks. Many of our phone conversations in the last years dealt with campus politics—he ranted and raved. I introduced him to the gem dealer Karen Sinizer, who was his resource for all the unusual faceted stones he used in his last body of work, and we shopped for stones together two or three times a year. We talked about people in the jewelry and craft art world. After Vail stopped [the Summervail conferences, 1975–1985], I was probably the only peer in jewelry he had to talk with about this stuff.

"We discussed marriage several times, but unfortunately Ken never *asked* me, he always *told* me we should get married. But I knew I'd never keep growing as an artist in his shadow and I wanted a child. Ken really didn't want children. Ken was so much like his dad in hiding his emotions from most people. However, he really tried to be otherwise with me—maybe because I demanded it, who knows."

Theirs was a highly charged, dynamic, and long relationship. When Worden finally broke with Cory to go to Georgia, she left for good the Ellensburg she had grown up in, the Ellensburg that Ken Cory would never leave. "I had to break with everything," Worden says, "Ellensburg, the Northwest, Central, Ken. I was so young when I met him, and I didn't know anything else. I had to find my own voice. It was hard, but it was the most important thing I ever did." They remained extremely close, as friends and as professional peers, to the end of his life.

During a critique Ken might pick up a student's jewelry project and ask, "Would you pay fifty cents for this at a garage sale?" Years later, probably 1986, I was working as a commercial jeweler doing repairs. I used to haunt the flea markets and junk stores for replacement parts; rhinestones, fake pearls, stuff like that. Anyway, one day at a flea market I saw a box marked, EVERYTHING IN THIS BOX 25 CENTS. Lo and behold, I found the Idaho pin, a signed Pencil Brothers creation from 1972. I just about peed my pants. I paid my quarter and rushed home to call Ken; he laughed and laughed. Then about four years later, he called me and said, "Guess what? I just paid seventy-five cents for one of your pieces at the Salvation Army!"

—Nancy Worden

PENCIL BROTHERS
Idaho (pin), 1972
Enamel on gold-plated copper
1¾ × 1¼ × ¼ in.
Collection of Nancy Worden

Tompkins and Worden both mention Cory's teaching. He was by all accounts both an extremely generous and demanding teacher. Nancy Worden describes his teaching this way: "Our job was to find our own voice and he considered it his job to guide us in the formal aspects of technique, composition, and design. He was a harsh critic and that was hard for some people. He tried to train us to be disciplined thinkers as well as good craftsmen. He was the only studio teacher I had in eight years of college that made us think through our ideas like you would write a paper with many drafts. You'd show him an idea in your sketchbook and he'd say, 'That's a good start, now go do twenty thumbnail sketches on that theme.'

"He gave interesting conceptual assignments. I remember one was to go look at some Native American jewelry in the library and then design a contemporary piece using the Indian jewelry as inspiration, something he did many times in his own work. Another time the assignment was to design a tattoo for Kathy, the Art Department secretary. She was a lot of fun and an Elvis fan when it wasn't cool, but she was a terrible typist. I don't remember my design, but I remember Ken's was ELVIS spelled with a typo."

LePere, Tompkins, and Worden are the people Ken Cory allowed the closest into his life and art. Les LePere, a working graphic artist, and Cory were best friends and partners. Merrily Tompkins is an active and well-known Seattle artist. Nancy Worden is the only one of Cory's students to have made a full and successful career in metalsmithing and the arts, living today in Seattle and teaching at the Pratt Fine Arts Center. Together, the three comprised a kind of second family for Cory.

The Sacred in the Commonplace

The Graphic and Narrative Work, 1971–1975

"It cost me five bucks to ride the train to see Ken," LePere says, "and he would pick me up at the train station. We would make stuff all weekend. My fingers would be printless from all the time spent with a grinding stone smoothing our champlevé enamel pieces. Decorated, functional objects found their way into our art. Ken's house would be an egg-beatered array after one of these work-play sessions. Often the highlight would be a trip to the river or mountains to picnic and observe the world around us. Sometimes we took

PENCIL BROTHERS
Mix-n-Match Dude Ranch (belt buckle), 1974
Brass, enamel on copper, and found object
2¾ in. diameter × ¾ in. deep
Collection of Don Shiffman

wire and string to make little icons in the woods and we just left them there.

"The odd happening, the strange combination, and the very real notion that so many experiences were *beyond* natural became our reality. And then we found that other people liked our work. Ken was teaching and I was teaching at the Factory of Visual Arts so we didn't have to sell these creations of ours, so we put high prices on them and started to show them all over the U.S. and in England."

At this time, LePere was doing some cartooning for the *Seattle Flag*, an underground newspaper, signing himself "Pencil." "One weekend Ken showed me the enamel emblem of a Dodge truck radiator," LePere remembers. "It said 'Dodge Brothers, Detroit USA.' We had been enameling a circular buckle and I said 'Maybe we should be the Pencil Brothers.' Ken said, 'Yeah, you could be Lead and I could be Red. Better Red than Lead' he would say." The Pencil Brothers was born. They made enameled copper belt buckles and switch plates, ashtrays, and wall pieces together. From the early 1970s on through the decade, though they did make the two last Pencil Brothers pieces in 1986, they created over fifty pieces and exhibited in more than one hundred shows. The intensity and quality of this collaboration is unusual in American art, and their work belies the prevailing Modernist myth of the purely individualist artist. "How can two artists work together on one thing?" LePere asks rhetorically. "We said that no one questioned the validity of a jazz band." In his work as one of the Pencil Brothers, Cory was fully collaborating with LePere as a partner, and also at the same time

Broken Window (pin), 1972
Silver, copper, brass, and African
trade bead
3¼ × 1¼ × ½ in.

Les LePere and Ken Cory at the Ellensburg train station, mid-1970s

living alone, and intensely involved in teaching, making his own art, and studying technique and materials.

The Pencil Brothers' and Cory's independently crafted champlevé enameled copper works are all narrative-based art,[19] that is, each work tells a story, or has elements of storytelling infused in its arrangement of images. Each work was a picture-story, composed pictorially, as if the pieces had first been drawings and then were rendered in metal and enamel. All the works are top-loaded with puns, parody, satire, private jokes, and (often) sexual allusions. Among the best works from this time are the Pencil Brothers' *Camel* and *Train* (1971), *Texas* (1972), *Mix-n-Match Dude Ranch*, and the *Bird* and *Fish* pendants (1974), *Match* (an ashtray of 1976), and *Skunk* (1977). Then there was Cory's independent work, including *Broken Window* (1972), *Flats Fixed*, and the *Self Portrait* buckle (both 1975), an intriguing series of American Indian inspired works from 1974–76 including *Squash Blossom Necklace*, *TIN NUTS* (an acronym for "There Is Nothing New Under The Sun"), and *Autumn Sunset*; an amazing run of belt buckles in 1976 including *High Heel*, *Admit One*, *Field*, *Route 66*, and *How to Fix Your Snake*; and finally, *Nancy's Buckle* (a belt buckle of 1978) and the pin *V8* (1979).

The mystical tradition of the number 5[20] is present in much of this work. Five: earth, air, fire, water, void, or self. And the colors red, yellow, blue, white, black. The collision of the sacred and the commonplace. The sacred in the

PENCIL BROTHERS
Train (wall piece), 1971
Chrome-plated brass, copper, glass, enamel, and colored pencil drawing
4¼ × 3½ × ½ in.
Collection of Dennis Hadley

everyday. Notice how many of the buckles and wall pieces use a four-cornered composition with the void in the center, or a circular format which still evokes the four-cornered picture plane. The symbol 5 is mystical and sexual at once. The void is the center, the unknown, the mystery, for men, of the yoni, the vagina. Cory and LePere used this concept consciously as a tool for both the compositional framework of the works and as intellectual underpinning—they were fascinated by its history and its implications in their own lives and art. It is especially present in *Camel*, *Frame*, *Flats Fixed*, *Nancy's Buckle*, and to a lesser degree but present nonetheless, in *Broken Window* and *High Heel*—conceptually, the window is an evocative visual metaphor with its natural four-cornered structure and the emptiness, the inside and the outside, in its center.

Here are LePere's shorthand explanations for the stories behind individual pieces: "*How to Fix Your Snake*, penis maintenance; *High Heel*, another relationship out the window; *Admit One*, going through the proper channels in order to share sex; *Route 66*, close to a '69' California-style; *Field*, another set of tits out on the landscape, danger sign, always beware; *Frame*, all corners of a positive nature point toward the void, male toward female; *Train*, homage to our frequent viewing of 'landscape snakes' and the joy of them in the Kittitas Valley."

"One of the keys to all of the P. Boys work," LePere says, "was the goal of achieving a balance, the result of combining opposites: male-female, frame-picture, yang-yin, black-white, soft-hard, man-made/natural, geometric-organic, hot-cold, static-directional." Cory said the pencil is "the American yin-yang symbol—creative on one end, destructive on the other."[21]

PENCIL BROTHERS
Camel (wall piece), 1971
Enamel on copper, glass, and colored pencil drawing
4 × 4 × ¼ in.
Collection of Leslie LePere

One of the earliest Pencil Brothers pieces was *Camel*. "Ken and I," LePere says, "had made a couple of wall pieces as the 'Art Team' where we planned the collaboration of the frame and the picture, the outside and the inside, the yin and the yang. Our attractions to plays on words yielded 'camelflage' from camouflage. Ken sent me the frame with a camel cutout and with essentially no directions to go on but a camel picture insert, or, as it turned out, a camelflage inside. Put your wiener in a fire and get it warmed up. Get the point?"

The *Bird* and *Fish* pendants have a personal story behind them. Two Seattle women, the writers and art collectors Marcella Benditt and Marion Gartler (who sometimes called themselves the "Pencil Sisters"), were at the time writing textbooks together for junior high students with limited vocabularies. They had seen the Pencil Brothers' *Texas* (1972), that piece with the marvelous pencil frame and double-sharpened pencil set at the top, at the University of Washington's Henry Gallery in a group show. Marion commissioned Cory and LePere to make a pair of necklaces, and she gave *Fish* to Marcella as a gift. LePere says, "These ladies had a stream of ideas on a constant basis (thoughts), thus the ability in the pendants to rotate the center ring on each piece and change the pencil drawing—seen at the top in the bubble above the bird and fish—in the thought bubble. The pencils we included in the pendants were actually used by Marcella and Marion on their manuscripts; they did all their writing with pencils."

And another story, though neither LePere, Tompkins, nor Worden can confirm this: *How to Fix Your Snake* may be based on an old American Indian Trickster story,[22] the one in which Coyote,

PENCIL BROTHERS
Bird (pendant), 1974 (above)
Fish (pendant), 1974 (below)
Enamel on copper, glass beads,
graphite drawing, and Plexiglas
5½ × 3½ × ½ in. each
Bird Collection of Marion Gartler
Fish Collection of Marcella Benditt

spying a beautiful Princess bathing with her friends in a river, is consumed with lust. Coyote cuts off his penis and instructs it to swim out to the Princess and enter her for his pleasure—Trickster has plenty of magic for this kind of shenanigans. It doesn't work out well for Trickster in the end. If Cory knew this story—he read

How to Fix Your Snake (belt buckle), 1976
Brass, and enamel on copper
2¾ in. diameter × ½ in. deep
Whereabouts unknown

eclectically and broadly all his life—he is here making a reference to it. If he didn't, it is fascinating to think about the chance resonance in *How to Fix Your Snake* with an old and enduring North American oral tradition.

Flats Fixed and *Mix-n-Match Dude Ranch* come directly out of Cory's love for the emblematic in jewelry and in American advertising and popular culture—he actively collected enameled emblems and product signs of all kinds—like the enameled Dodge Brothers car ornament he and LePere had been looking at when they took the Pencil Brothers name. *Flats Fixed* pays direct homage to that specific ornament, to the tradition in American manufacturing and advertising, and also works in the compositional element of the number 5, though here rather simply and straightforwardly.

The Pencil Brothers' works are full of all that *stuff* they both loved from American consumer culture: pencils—always pencils, after all, the essential tool they shared—playing cards, pool balls and dominoes, rocket ships, toasters, elements of the eastern Washington landscape and rural culture they grew up in, desert landscapes, birds, animals. Snakes, sticks and branches, trains thrusting outward from the picture plane, the rear ends of dairy cows. And naked women. Theirs is essentially boys' work, boys' imagery, punningly dirty, smutty, rebellious. Some of it silly, yes, but the best is provocative and trenchant

Flats Fixed (belt buckle), 1975
Brass, enamel on copper, and silver
2 × 2¾ × ¾ in.

PENCIL BROTHERS
Skunk (wall piece), 1977
Enamel on copper, Plexiglas, ink drawing,
and wood
4 × 4 × ½ in.
Collection of Leslie LePere

PENCIL BROTHERS
Blimp (wall piece), 1971
Enamel on copper, Plexiglas, and colored pencil
and ink drawing
4 × 4 × 1 in.
Collection of Helen Drutt

PENCIL BROTHERS
Egypt (wall piece), 1974
Enamel on copper, glass, graphite drawing, and
wood
4 × 4 × ½ in.
Collection of Leslie LePere

and funny. And the Pencil Brothers' jewelry and Cory's independent work of this time is primarily jewelry for men, not at all common, yet, in the jewelry world.

The series of narrative buckles that Cory created independently, but in harmony with the Pencil Brothers work—*How to Fix Your Snake, Route 66, High Heel,* and *Admit One*—are like snapshots, momentary picture-stories caught *in medias res* and on the fly, in which the viewer feels at home, drawn in, part of the narrative, comfortable with all those recognizable, telling details and objects from popular culture and the West. What just happened? What happens next? What does the desert floor covered with oranges mean, and where is the candy-apple red coupe going? Few metalsmiths or jewelers of this time—save Don Tompkins and others using vernacular imagery, like Noma Copley, Fred Woell, Bob Ebendorf, Lane Coulter—were making work like these story-telling, content-laden, trickster-like enameled copper works.

In all this graphically narrative, iconographic, iconoclastic, spiritually resonant, and often comic work, LePere and Cory created a rich, multilayered group of objects that constantly piqued the social, sexual, and aesthetic mores of the time,

PENCIL BROTHERS
Match (ashtray), 1976
Enamel on copper
5¾ in. diameter × ¾ in. deep
Collection of Don Shiffman

and which often explored both a highly developed personal set of references and old mystical traditions. They also made an art fully grounded in the West—theirs is an unselfconsciously regional aesthetic, fully grown from where they lived and what they lived with. LePere and Cory were poking fun at all this Western American ethos: the small towns they'd gone to school in, the rigid sexual and social mores of the 1950s and early 1960s, the dominant aesthetics the West inherited from the East Coast. At the same time, they were honoring the things they loved: cars, girls' bodies—they still called women "girls" then—bar games, board games, the landscape, the natural world, and the presence, the functional elegance, of the well-used machinery and farm outbuildings

High Heel (belt buckle), 1976
Enamel on copper and brass
2¾ in. diameter × ½ in. deep

Admit One (belt buckle), 1976
Enamel on copper and brass
2¾ in. diameter × ½ in. deep

Route 66 (belt buckle), 1976
Enamel on copper and brass
2¾ in. diameter × ½ in. deep

scattered on the Palouse. They were honoring the place where they lived. Even now, eastern Washington is a region of small villages, of neon-decorated drive-in hamburger joints, a place with a few remaining single- and double-pump gas stations where fan belts and radiator hoses hang from the ceiling on S hooks, a landscape where generations of used-up farm machinery sit along washes and creek banks silently decaying into the landscape. Mary Hu says, "There was a time in the 1970s when everyone was making geometric-based work ["Scandinavian-slick," she calls it]. Ken was doing the narrative pieces then and there were so few working that way. And in all this work there is a sense of place. Very few metalsmiths do work that is about and from the place they live. He knew the West was marginalized. But it was *his place*."[23]

During this period Cory was studying American Indian jewelry and beading traditions, especially Columbia Plateau beaded bags and clothing, and Pacific Northwest Coast and Southwest iconography and metalsmithing techniques. He made a few things that are blatant copies of traditional Native American forms or images—an engraved buckle and bracelet with traditional Northwest Indian designs (not dated) and the *Redwing* buckle (1975) are the best examples here. Sometimes when he did simply copy traditional forms or others' images—his way of studying and teaching himself the techniques—he signed them "Ellen X. Redheart"[24] or with a heart-shaped stamp, as an homage, a kind of joke, and so as not to confuse us that this is *Ken Cory's* original work. Three original works that did evolve from this exploration are pivotal ones: the *Squash Blossom Necklace*, which he made for Merrily Tompkins; the *TIN NUTS* necklace, and the most important of these, *Autumn Sunset*. All incorporate historical techniques—the traditional form of the Hopi squash

Redwing (belt buckle), 1975
Brass and glass beads on leather
2¾ × 3½ × ¾ in.

Autumn Sunset (aka **Candy Corn**) (belt buckle), 1975
Sterling silver and laminated acrylic
2½ in. diameter × ½ in. deep

TIN NUTS (There Is Nothing New Under The Sun)
(necklace), 1975
Silver, brass, wood, mirror, and glass beads on
leather
27 × 2½ × 1½ in.

blossom necklace; the use of seed beads in the Mexican-inspired *TIN NUTS*; and the traditional (that is, at least back to 1939) Hopi overlay metalsmithing techniques, design, composition, and iconography of *Autumn Sunset*. In these works Cory created an adroit collision between Native American techniques and forms, and a satiric, ironic, and ultimately hilarious commentary on American consumer culture and the trendy, Southwestern Indian jewelry and art so popular then and today. In these pieces, he challenged both his peers in the jewelry community and the audience—the buyers—of contemporary and traditional Native American work. He was making, and having, a lot of fun.

Composed of empty .22 rifle shells, small light bulbs, and a cast-

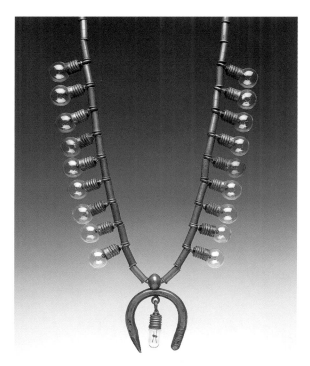

Squash Blossom Necklace, 1974
Brass, leather, and found objects
15¼ × 7½ × ¾ in.
Collection of Merrily Tompkins

bronze pencil curved like a crescent moon, *Squash Blossom Necklace* is irreverently funny and tender all at once. A bison with a triangle of mirror on its body hangs from the beaded cord in *TIN NUTS*. And then there is *Autumn Sunset*, in which an authentically traditional Hopi overlay design in silver surrounds six pieces of laminated-plastic Halloween candy corn. Lane Coulter and Jan Brooks, peers of Cory's—Coulter is an authority on Native American jewelry—remember the work well. Brooks says, "You don't have to be versed in the politics of culture when you look at this thing to understand . . . the specific reference to Native American work. And then you get the candy corn in there as an American Halloween ritual . . . it is this whole cultural collage." Coulter says, "Everywhere, if you were teaching or dealing with jewelry at that time, it was impossible to avoid, you had to meet it head on, the whole notion of Indian jewelry, because it was in every truck stop in America at that point. And Ken understood that and made a piece that had to do with that as its subject."

Sometime during 1971, when Cory was living in the Mad House, he made the eccentric, quirky paperweight *Monument to Katie Moon* with copper, brass, silver, lead, enamel, and leather. In 1975 he made his *Self Portrait* belt buckle with cast bronze and found objects under resin. Nancy Worden suggests *Katie Moon* is strongly influenced by Kenneth Patchen's *Journal of Albion Moonlight*,[25] that Beat/ Surrealist masterpiece which Cory read as a student. The piece includes a small naked woman trapped under a tiny glass bell jar. The glass is *screwed* down under

Monument to Katie Moon (paperweight), 1971
Lead, copper, brass, silver, enamel, glass, and found object
1½ × 2¼ × 1½ in.

a metal armature and a strand of twisted silver wire loops down from a wall-like edifice behind the woman and sprawls over a chess board. Lying on the chess board is an organic tongue shape, covered with silver granulations. At the four corners of the paperweight are brass screws. It is a static, Surrealist stage. *Self Portrait* is more densely loaded: trapped under the resin there is a die rolled to the number 5; a well-used pencil; an unshelled peanut; a single ticket stub which reads "Admit One"; a small, elegant, empty, stoppered glass vial; a piece of rough turquoise; a zinc-coated steel penny dated 1943, the year Cory was born; an unlit kitchen match; a big-bellied number 5; and some beads. There's too much mystery in these pieces to try to decipher them, but here, present again, are all the major intellectual and aesthetic interests that Cory sifted through during his whole career: specific, precise, highly personalized images and objects; a continuing fascination with the role, the presence, the power, and the visual *meaning* of objects in his life; the mystery of the number 5; an engagement with the craft of metalsmithing and its materials; the dynamic collision of different materials; the pencil and all that it signifies—sex and danger and desire.

"We were recording our own histories in these things," Les LePere says, speaking of their collaborations, but insightful regarding Cory's independent work. "We were recording our thoughts, our lives. We made the thing to figure out what we were interested in. It wasn't the end, just making the

(Untitled) Self Portrait (belt buckle), 1975
Cast bronze, cast resin, and found objects
2½ × 2½ × ¾ in.

buckle or whatever, it was the beginning, a way to explore what it was that interested us. We wanted to make something functional, recognizable, and we wanted to have fun. And we wanted to explore the sacred in the commonplace."

By the mid-1970s their work together began to significantly slow down. "After I moved to the farm in 1981," LePere says, "we would see each other a couple of times a year. I realized that in order for any more shared work to happen, it rested on my shoulders. Only a couple more were made after 1981. But we never outgrew the directions we took in our work together."

Fireworks

Summervail, 1975–1985

In the summer of 1975, the metalsmiths Jim Cotter and Lane Coulter created the Rocky Mountain Metalsmithing Symposium, part of the summer school program at Colorado Mountain College in Vail—also called, in its early years, the Summer Vail Workshop for Art and Critical Studies. Eventually, metalsmiths simply called it "Summervail." It was a shoestring operation in its first few years, but became a dynamic and fertile meeting place for American metalsmiths. Lane Coulter had seen Cory's work in the *Objects: USA* catalogue and several issues of *Craft Horizons*, and tells the story of inviting Cory to that first conference this way: "When Cotter and I made up the notion of the Summervail Metal Symposium, we invited everybody we knew, which wasn't very many, but we were shooting to get maybe ten people and we asked a couple of people that we didn't know. And the two that I remember particularly were Ken Cory and Gary Noffke, from Georgia."

Jan Brooks adds, "Sometime in the late 60s, I remember seeing Ken's work pictured in probably *Craft Horizons*.[26] And I'm sure I remember his work from the Johnson's Wax catalogue. I don't remember which year that was, but I remember seeing the work and remembering Ken's name and being very impressed with what he was up to. You see, he was one of the youngest people included in that show and there was this picture in there of him in his car. And I thought, ah . . .

First Summervail Symposium, 1975
Left to right: J. Fred Woell, Elliot Pujol, Ken Cory, Lane Coulter, Al Pine,
Lynda Watson, Jim Cotter, Joe Atteberry, Harold O'Connor, Dan Teleen
Photographer unknown

this is cool because he wasn't that much older than I was, whereas he's in this show with my teacher, Brent Kington." Lane Coulter says, "The piece I remember in particular was one that has a kind of a stuffed leather tongue sticking out of it and I think it's also a cast copper piece [*Tongue*]. And so when I met him then at Summervail, I learned that my original perceptions of this guy and his work were pretty accurate, that what he was doing was not related to all these things I was hearing and seeing in the metal field, that Cory was working with stuff from somewhere else. What I learned, meeting him and working with him all those summers at Vail, was, in fact, that he did have this strong West Coast interest in machinery and cars, car culture for sure. I mean, I saw that stuffed leather tongue detail on that little piece as being like upholstery, like car upholstery. You know, tuck-and-roll upholstery. That's what made me sit up and pay attention to his pieces. I didn't know who he was, but I knew that he was really up to something unrelated to what I had seen in the field and that he went about it in a totally different way than anybody else that I knew of at the time.

"I managed to find out where Ken lived," Coulter says, "and I called. He didn't have a phone at home for a number of years, so I called him at school and invited him to this symposium and he asked a lot of questions about what he was supposed to do and what we were doing, and it was a little hard to answer because we'd never done one. And I asked him about doing

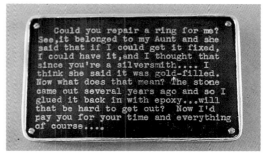

LANE COULTER
Repair Work Buckle, 1980
Brass, copper, and tin
2¾ × 4⅜ × ¾ in.
Collection of Michael Croft

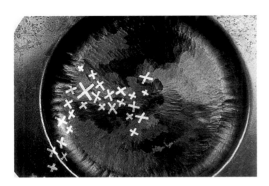

JAN BROOKS
Collection Plate # 3; Cat Food, 1979
Sterling silver and mild steel
12 in. diameter × 1½ in. deep
Collection of Richard Quinnell

demonstrations and lectures and things like that, and he said, well, he'd never done one before and I said, why not? And he said nobody had ever asked him."

Cory taught at the first Summervail conference, had a great time, returned to teach the next summer with Merrily Tompkins, and attended every summer until the conferences ended in 1985. Summervail was his chance to load up the MG, roll out of the isolation of central Washington, and take his time driving the back roads between Ellensburg and Vail. At the Summervail Conference he could spend three to nine weeks, intense weeks by all accounts, with people he liked, with people who liked him and his work, with people who were developing the same interests he had already been exploring in jewelry for more than a decade. For the metal community, and especially for Cory, naturally reclusive and living in Ellensburg, Summervail was a powerful communal force. The conference allowed people to meet each other, make friendships, and share ideas and skills. It infused the community with all the still-unleashed—at least in the early years—potential of new materials, techniques, forms, and surfaces in jewelry. Many of the then-young metalsmiths who would go on to make good work and to teach in university metal programs attended off and on or regularly over its history: Coulter and Cotter of course, Gary Noffke, Lynda Watson-Abbott, Elliot Pujol, Jan Brooks, Bob Ebendorf, Mary Hu, and many others.

This is how Coulter describes the time, and Cory's influence on metalsmithing, during the Summervail years: "Everybody that got into making jewelry during that period was doing it

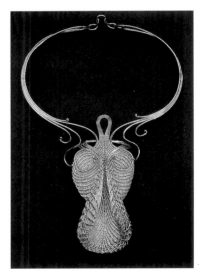

MARY LEE HU
Choker # 41, 1978
Fine and sterling silver, and 18K gold
9½ × 6½ × 1 in.
Private collection

in sort of a reactionary way and then eventually realized that it really was a profession and something you did, and so all sorts of people, Ken included, got real interested in the techniques, but not so much for themselves, not just for the technique, but using it for their own personal reasons, very specific personal reasons. Like Ken didn't know diddley about setting stones, but he sat down and taught himself how to do it. And he probably asked people who knew how to do it, and he took the time to learn it right. Because he was a jeweler, he was also an art teacher, but he was a jeweler, and he maintained that interest very specifically so that if he wanted to make something that involved a technique that he didn't know how to do, he'd just go learn how to do it and incorporate it. But, and this is the important part, he did it for the purpose of making some design element

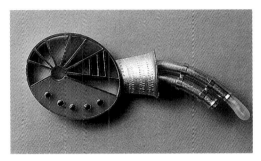

ROBERT EBENDORF
Wheel of Fortune (brooch), 1975
Silver, gold plate, Plexiglas, pearl, sapphires, and rubies
1 × 2½ × ¼ in.
Private collection

that he wanted to make, not to show off the fact that he knew how to do it."

Jan Brooks says it this way: "There were people at Summervail who considered themselves primarily designers. And I remember feeling opposition to that. And Ken, I wouldn't have categorized him that way. He wasn't someone I would call a designer. Cory is a cultural commentator, because in all his work he borrows from all this stuff around him, and there's this strong content in the work. And yes, it's well-designed, but the thoughts in it speak much more loudly than any sort of self-consciously designed thing. When you talked to him, he was so intense. You could have a conversation with him that would be full of humor, humor that was really clever, humor that was not shallow, humor that was really, really clever, incredibly intelligent. Full of parody. You would be telling him something, and he would answer with a question and it was always . . . well, it was like looking at his work. His pieces would ask a question and answer it at the same time."

Lynda Watson-Abbott, long a teacher of metalsmithing at Cabrillo College in Aptos, California, says, "Summervail in the early 70s was a place to let loose socially and creatively. Most (or many) of us did a year's worth of partying in the weeks

As Lane Coulter mentions, technique-for-technique's-sake was not necessarily the heart of the work metalsmiths did together at the Summervail conferences. A tradition did develop, though, that is purely "techo-weenie" (his words) in its origins, and that became the "Olympic Games" of Summervail—the Saw, File, and Solder Sprints. How it was played says a lot about this generation's ability to have fun as part of their making art.

Mary Hu, who attended Summervail several times, describes the annual event: "Three-person teams were formed and lined up at the starting line. The backfire from an oxyacetylene torch was the starting signal, and the first person in the team raced out to a table set with tools, put a sawblade into a sawframe and sawed a strip out of a four-inch square piece of copper sheet. It had to be long enough to be bent around to form a ring. Then the first person took the strip, ran back and gave it to the second team member who ran to the table, filed the strip where need-ed, bent it around a ring mandrel to form a ring, ran back, and handed it to the third team member. That person ran up, soldered the ring, pickled off the flux, and ran back. The ring had to fit one of the thirty fingers of the team members." Mary claims the record was under one minute—maybe two minutes.

we were in Colorado. Living in tents, sharing a bathroom, and eating every meal together made it a unique experience. Many of us who taught metalsmithing and jewelry at that time —particularly those of us on the West Coast and in rural areas, like Ken and me—felt geographically isolated from other jewelers and isolated within our own departments."

Gary Noffke first met Cory in a parking lot at CCAC in 1971, the year Cory was teaching there. Noffke observes that at this time, at the turn of the 1960s and throughout the 70s, the crafts were much closer than they are now. "The Funk movement was big in ceramics, glass, and metals, along with wood and fibers to a lesser degree, but all the craft areas were aware of each other. The important thing here is that influences were more open then. The glassblowers and ceramic people influenced Ken and he influenced them. The sort of work he was doing then was in its heyday. His work and his collaborations with Les LePere were always in the forefront, not only at the height of Funk but in the larger crafts revival of the time.

"I also believe Ken was more observant of the other art forms—drawing, painting, sculpture—than most of his contemporaries. A lot of Ken's work is very similar to mine. We both had a deep contempt for the 'cutting edge' look in any art form. We mastered certain techniques as we needed them, not because they

LYNDA WATSON-ABBOTT
Sheep Bracelet, 1974
Sterling silver and acrylic enamel
3 × 4 × ¾ in.
Whereabouts unknown

were popular. Ideas were important. We were both rebels, to the limits of what our academic positions would tolerate. We were relentless in showing our contempt for our own colleagues and contemporaries who were set on making art-looking stuff. We made fun of everyone and everything—usually well enough and subtly enough not to piss them off too much."

Because Summervail succeeded in bringing together metalsmiths from throughout the country, especially bringing the East Coast people to the West, and because they got to know each other, learned from and taught

each other, slept together and drank beer and smoked pot together those weeks each summer in Colorado all through the mid-1970s and into the mid-1980s, Cory influenced many of the top metalsmiths working then, just as they influenced him, and the results spread across the country.

GARY NOFFKE
Set of Spoons, late 1970s
Silver, steel, and tin-plated copper
Largest approx. 8 × 3 × 1 in.
Collection of the artist

Bridge

The Research Period, 1979–1986

Cory had few close friends in the CWU Art Department, though he liked Connie Speth and William Dunning, who was often the good-natured brunt of Cory's practical jokes. During these years he was close with two of his best students, Frank Samuelson and Charlie King, who were around his house a great deal. He was friends, but not close, with artists Dick Elliott and Jane Orleman.[27] And of course he remained close with LePere, Tompkins, and Worden. He was in Ellensburg though, isolated geographically and spiritually.

Between 1979 and 1986 Cory made very little jewelry, though he continued to work, and did make four pieces we must consider closely here—*Nancy's Buckle* (1978); *V8* (1979); the *101 Twisted Wires* (1979–81); and *Metamorphosis* (1981). It is clear that he went through a long dry spell—nearly eight years—beginning in the late 1970s. Nearly a decade in the life of an artist who lived only fifty years is significant. What happened? The Pencil Brothers collaboration was over. Perhaps he was bored. As inventive as the Pencil Brothers work was—it is greatly admired both by metalsmiths and historians in the field—Cory may have grown tired or frustrated with the form, with the enameling process. It was a period of introspection, very possibly of questions about his work—what artist doesn't suffer doubts?—and of study and intense research.

The period was clearly a transition for Cory. He perhaps didn't know where he was going next with his work. He was thinking, drawing—there

Measuring Spoons, 1979
Sterling silver
5 × 5½ × ¾ in.
Collection of Beverly Cory

(Untitled) Wooden Table, 1980
Painted wood
51 × 40 × 31 in.
Collection of Beverly Cory

Functional objects
Frame, 1992; silver and glass, 3 × 2¼ × ⅓ in. **Tape Dispenser,** 1993; sterling
silver, wood, and steel; 1¾ × 3½ × 1¾ in. **Notebook,** 1986; sterling silver, steel,
and paper; 5 × 3¼ × ½ in. **Jeweler's Loupe,** 1985; sterling silver and glass;
1½ × 1 × ½ in. **Comb,** 1987; sterling silver; 4½ × 1 × ¼ in. **Ruler,** 1989; silver, and
enamel on copper; 6 × ¾ × ⅛ in. **Letter Opener,** 1979; brass, and enamel on
copper; 6¾ × 1 × ¼ in.
Collection of Beverly Cory

is no appreciable gap in the sketchbooks—experimenting with new techniques, inventing some tools, still visiting Summervail each summer, though not as a teacher. He was working on his house and also making some technically interesting but ultimately minor works. In 1980, for example, there was *Cupcake Box*, a test he gave himself, an exact replica in copper of a Hostess cupcake. He went down and bought one to compare only *after* he had completed his—it is perfect, by the way. Then *Tape Measure*, which some guess is his portrait of two women mad at him. And finally *Wooden Table*, his delightfully whimsical dining table with its snake, pencil, branch, and rope legs.

"Probably his period of limited work, assuming he had one," Gary Noffke says, "was spent thinking about subject matter—not technique or any 'popular look of the day' format. But, whatever he did or didn't do in that period was a result of deep intellectual thought and personal reflection. I would guess most artists of any importance occasionally think more than they work." Noffke has it right. Cory began working on jewelry again toward the end of 1985.

Tape Measure (side one), ca. 1980
Sterling silver, turquoise, garnet, bone, and steel tape
2 × 2 × ¾ in.
Collection of Beverly Cory

Tape Measure (side two), ca. 1980
Sterling silver, turquoise, garnet, bone, and steel tape
2 × 2 × ¾ in.
Collection of Beverly Cory

But first: in 1978 Cory made *Nancy's Buckle* for Nancy Worden, a millefiore-style, sterling, copper, brass, and enamel belt buckle. It is one of the few buckles he ever made for a woman. Using the same concept that the Venetian glassblowers developed for glass, Cory made bundles of different-colored metal rods, encased them in tubing, and then sliced off sections. The sections were then laid out in his desired design, soldered together on a single sheet, and the excess solder ground off to reveal the pattern. At the time, there may not have been any other metalsmiths using this technique. Not only is the piece unique, stunning, and beautiful—the bird in flight with images

One piece of Ken's that comes to mind was the millefiori belt buckle he made for Nancy Worden. He copied the glass-blowers who made thousands of pounds of millefiori beads, also the Romans, and maybe others before them, who made sheet glass out of them and slumped them in bowl forms. It was a bit of technical genius, as Ken made his own drawplates with various configurations, bundled the drawn wires, soldered them together in various metals and patterns, then sawed thin slices and soldered them into a sheet for fabrication. Actually, I don't know if he was making fun of the process or honoring it.

—Gary Noffke

(Untitled) Nancy's Buckle, 1978
Silver, copper, brass, cloisonné enamel, and mirror
2¼ × 3 × ½ in.
Collection of Nancy Worden

seemingly floating on its body; the use of the number 5 compositional strategy again, with its brass markers at the four corners and the bird flying into that mystical void; and the small circular mirror in the center, the heart—*Nancy's Buckle* is also haunting, one of the last narrative works, and an intensely private, visual poem.

V8, from 1979, is cloisonné enamel on fine silver, as well as a piece of twist-ed wire and a small, round carnelian stone. It is technically interesting—

V8 (pin), 1979
Silver, enamel, and carnelian
2 × 2¼ × ¼ in.

the enamel here is particularly exquis-ite, a West African basket or Navajo pot–like pattern makes the snake's scales seem almost alive—but in the end *V8*, with its emblematic reference and pretty obvious pun, is far less reso-nant than *Nancy's Buckle*.

The two works that are essential to understanding this period of transi-tion and the works which followed are 10: *Twisted Wires* and the *Metamorphosis*

(Untitled) Cupcake Box, 1980
Copper and silver
1½ × 2¾ in. diameter

101 Twisted Wires (detail), 1979–1981
Copper wire
6 × ⅛ in. diameter

bracelet. These works lead, in different but compelling ways, to the last work.

In Herbert Maryon's famous old classic metalsmithing technical manual, *Metalwork and Enamelling,* Maryon illustrates how to create unique patterns of twisted wire for incorporation into jewelry. Sometime in 1979, apparently as a self-imposed problem to solve, Cory set about creating a collection of new twisted wire designs—more than Maryon had created was the goal, like setting a new record. Cory used his rolling mill and drawplates, some of them homemade, created out of old truck springs which he annealed, drilled, and filed out. Some patterns are a single wire twisted and/or rolled, other patterns are two or more wires combined. When he finished, there were 101 different twisted wires in his group. The prominent Seattle jewelry artist, Kiff Slemmons, says, "I remember well when Ken showed me this piece. They were in a glass jar sticking up, no lid. He dumped them out on the table like pick-up sticks and that is close to how I picked them up—extracting them, one by one from the pile, examining each variation with more and more wonder—an experience of progressive wonder—the warmth of the copper, the organic quality, their seemingly endless variety, the sound they made. And then thinking 'What an idea!' To do all these sticks, yet another part of Ken: the con-

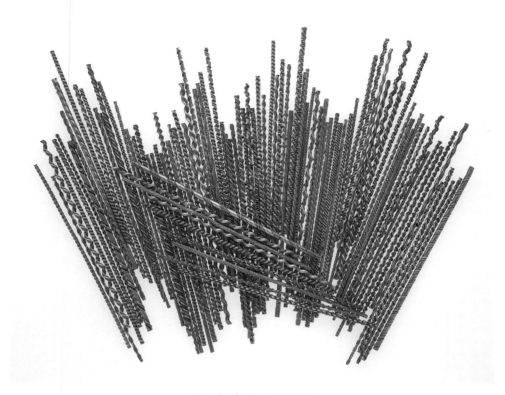

101 Twisted Wires, 1979–1981
Copper wire and glass jar
Wires 6 × ⅛ in. diameter

nection of 'science,' the spirit of investigation, of possibilities, experiment. Somehow in Ken's hands the whole endeavor had an elegance to it, a kind of elegance of concept and execution, and yet the scale of it was so important, the smallness, the detail, everything so closely examined."

Cory had learned how Native Americans in the Southwest used to forge spoons from silver dollars. This inspired the making of *Metamorphosis*, a bracelet of twelve 1981 copper pennies on a silver chain (1981 was the last year of the copper penny). It is the true bridge to the final works Cory began late in 1986. Here Cory begins with a single untouched penny. He then progresses around the bracelet through eleven steps, progressively hammering out the copper until by the twelfth penny there is no longer a penny at all but an exquisite, finished copper spoon. Kiff Slemmons suggests that this is a fully postmodern work. She observes that, like the California conceptual artist John Baldessari sharpening his pencil, in this piece all the process is open and acknowledged, demystified, leaving us in the

Metamorphosis (bracelet), 1981
Copper and silver
9 × 2½ × ¼ in.

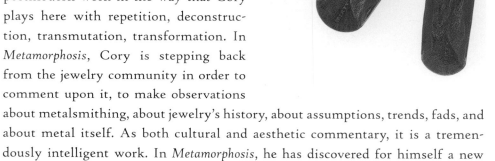

presence of a deep poignancy of transformation, a metaphor for art—a penny into a spoon. *Metamorphosis* is a postmodern work in the way that Cory plays here with repetition, deconstruction, transmutation, transformation. In *Metamorphosis*, Cory is stepping back from the jewelry community in order to comment upon it, to make observations about metalsmithing, about jewelry's history, about assumptions, trends, fads, and about metal itself. As both cultural and aesthetic commentary, it is a tremendously intelligent work. In *Metamorphosis*, he has discovered for himself a new relationship to the object, to material, to process.

Five years later, beginning sometime in 1986 and continuing with terrific force right through 1994, he began making a large new group of work.

Last Works
1986–1994

Between late 1986 and his death in 1994, Cory made just under two dozen last works, all pins.[28] Among the best are: *Face*, *Architecture*, *Arm*, *Bear*, *Coffee*, *Boat*, *Table*, *Sign*, *Whip*, *Dress*, *Tent*, *Arches*, *Satellite*, *Knows*, *Fire*, *Landscape*, *Beach*, and the last, *Peanut*. Although they are like and yet unlike anything Cory had yet done, these pins, as the final coda in Ken Cory's art, are layered with kinship to his very first works. There is a full arc from the first significant works of 1967–68 to the last work, from *Tongue* to *Landscape*, from *Set of Five* to *Fire*, from the 1971 *Rope* to the 1988 *Whip*, from *Nipple* to *Knows* (he'd like that alliteration). The last pins are still grounded in the recognizable, the everyday object—the heart of his work as an artist—but more subtly and deftly abstracted. Some honor the machines he loved, others the land forms he knew so well. All the works honor history and technique in the jeweler's craft. Like virtually all his earlier work, the last pins are informed by his systematic junking and collecting, his close observation of the landscape, farm and small-town architecture, and his love of popular culture and its clutter. Throughout his life these are the essential gestures of his art. The pins are also all skewed, even if only slightly, so that what you think you see is sure to foil you, to delight you. "He took these forms from the natural world and the stuff around us," Les LePere says, "and created a secretive, private, associative kind of work that looked abstract but wasn't at all if you looked closely." The craft, techniques, and materials he used in the last work are simply the basic materials and tools of the traditional jeweler's workbench: silver and gold, semiprecious stones set beautifully, stamping, casting, masonite

These pieces are hard to make. In fact, it has taken me thirty years to get to the point where I can do work this fine. It takes days, weeks, or sometimes months to come up with an idea, develop and refine the design, and then construct the pieces with craftsmanship appropriate for the works of art. I figure that after the gallery takes their cut, I'm barely making minimum wage. So, if you buy my work you are getting a real good deal.

—Ken Cory, sometime in the mid-1980s

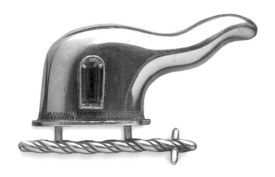

Bear (pin), 1987
Silver, 24K gold, 18K gold, and blue topaz
1¼ × 2 × ½ in.

Coffee (pin), 1987
Silver, 18K gold, malachite, and lapis
¾ × 1¾ × ½ in.

Sign (pin), 1988
Silver, copper, and 22K gold
2¼ × 1½ × ½ in.

die-forming. The results though, the images, are utterly original, all the more for their resonance within the history and tradition of metalsmithing, jewelry, and decoration.

Kiff Slemmons puts it this way: "Whenever I saw Ken's work over the years, it always lasted well beyond the immediate experience of seeing it in front of me. There was a subtlety and sense of irony that affected me strongly. I felt a kinship with his nonacademic leanings and his acute observations and intelligence. His work activated the mind as well as the senses—he always worked as an artist as well as a craftsman. The world of his work was larger than the world of jewelry alone, though he was especially acute in his references to jewelry as a medium itself and as expression in other cultures."

Table (pin), 1987
Silver, copper, 24K gold, 18K gold,
tourmaline, and rhodolite
1¼ × 1¼ × ½ in.

The last pins, that body of intellectual and material inquiry that he finally reached with the *Metamorphosis* breakthrough and then the Airstream trailer–inspired *Face*, have a source, a grounding in Funk, "retaining the mystery of Funk,"[29] but are Funk no longer. These last images come from the depths of his own voice, a voice free now of narrative. As much as historians may continue to place Ken Cory in the Funk tradition, these last works must be understood as something new, something there is yet no name for. They are the last startlingly original work of an artist who could have picked any material at all—oil and canvas, monumental cast bronze, or carved wood—but who instead chose to make sculpture in miniature, sculpture as jewelry, icon-like badges marking the way at each step in a lifelong dialogue with materials and techniques, with the culture he grew up in, with the sublime and mysterious world he watched so closely, an ongoing dialogue with

Tent (pin), 1988
Silver, 18K gold, and carnelian
¼ × 2½ × ½ in.

objects, with the things, the shapes, the presences that marked out meaning in his life and art.

There are too many pieces here to discuss them all in depth—this last decade's body of work was an extraordinary output. It is important, though, to look closely at a few, and to contrast the last pieces to his earliest works.

The Airstream trailer shows up in Cory's sketchbooks early and then floats in and out of the pages throughout his life. That squat, bulbous, beautiful-ugly shape is a visual metaphor for so many things American: pick up and go, the road trip, carry it on your back, the middle-class urge to recreate all the comforts of home any old place. It is but one of a large number of talismanic forms for Cory. *Face* is the Airstream trailer deftly abstracted. It is also a bear, a human being on all fours, a gateway. That odd little piece of faceted stone, andalusite here, set into its side is a gesture that he'll incorporate throughout these last works, a gesture that surprised all his peers who knew his earlier work. By no means the most successful piece in this group, it's a little out of balance, a bit unresolved with the twisted wire there at the bottom, that funny little copper projectile—nose? penis? digit? nipple?—sticking out the front. However tentative, *Face* is a new beginning. He must have known something was going on in it.

Face (pin), 1986
Copper, silver, 24K gold, 18K gold, and andalusite
1 × 1½ × ½ in.

The Airstream trailer motif appears even more clearly, and successfully, as the visual underpinning for the 1987 pin *Saw*. More refined, sleeker, and funnier than *Face*, *Saw* is composed of silver, brass, a garnet stone, a piece of twisted copper wire curved under the body, and the trailer hitch itself, also fashioned of copper. The shape of the sloping silver mass and the presence of the hitch make *Saw* the most visually literal of all these last pins. At the same time, it is saturated with other visual references: bug, beetle (like Volkswagon beetle), camp saw, breast, a Palouse hill, the horizon. And the hitch-like shape there at the front is, significantly, tongue, udder, finger, penis. To these last works, Cory is bringing his whole collection of nouns, what he called his *essential images*, all those *things* he had been accumulating, studying, and

Development sketch from Ken Cory Sketchbook No. 21, ca. 1988

Saw (pin), 1988
Silver, copper, and garnet
1¼ × 2 × ½ in.

drawing for the past thirty years and, layer by layer, incorporating them.

In 1988 he made *Arm* with sterling silver, 22K gold, copper, and garnet, and *Landscape* with 22K gold, sterling silver, and a really eccentric piece of faceted tourmaline. Both pieces are layered with organic and sexual references: the overall shape of both pieces so like hills and yet so like erotic bulging breasts, vulvas, scrota, or penises; the tiny breast-like forms at the bottom of *Arm*, the vulva-like slice in the center of *Landscape*. *Arm* repeats concerns he first explored in the 1969 *Shift* and 1970 *Levers*: his enduring fascination with machines, dynamic movement, and opposition, the tension between the organic and the man-made. *Landscape* is a reworking of 1967's *Wave* and *Reflector*, all three abstractions from the organic world, works about the landscape's physical presence and resonance, works about decay. In *Landscape* everything is now fully fluid, with a quiet, elegant evocation of opposites, tensions, and presences.

Fire (1988) incorporates the "mother image"—he never really left that one behind—and so reworks ideas he used in *Set of Five* and *Red Snake* from 1968. In 1968 there is the dripping, twisting, oozing red plastic shape hanging off the cast copper pyramid, and the levers resting in the centers in *Set of Five*. *Fire* incorporates an arm-like curve of silver with the small, round garnet at its end. What is this arm-like gesture? A salute? Hello? A quote from the jeweler's tradition? Whatever it is, it is whimsical, a technically complex and humorous way to draw attention to those set stones.

Those last pins, it's as if he made them not with a ten-speed bicycle but with a Harley Davidson motorcycle.

—Ruth Tamura

Whip (pin), 1988
Silver and smoky quartz
1¾ × 2¼ × ½ in.

The 1988 *Whip* and the 1971 *Rope* illustrate both how far these last works are from Funk and how intricately connected all his work is from the first period to the last. The two works are, in many ways, exactly the same piece. But in *Whip* all the elements are refined, honed, smoothed, completely in balance: the placement and gentle arc of the wire is simply beautiful the way it drapes and hangs there so lightly; the button or manhole-like shape evokes so much in the jeweler's decorative tradition; the weave-like stamping softens the silver's surface and the round smoky quartz stone resides there delightfully in opposition to the spigot-like shape it sits in. The earlier *Rope*, as good as it is for its own time, is cruder, harsher, less complete. With *Whip*, Cory has fully mastered scale, making this tiny pin monumental, making those few ounces of metal and stone *feel* massive, and at the same time giving weight, substance, and perfectly balanced mass to a miniature sculpture.

Satellite is the piece in this group which most reminds us of Cory's long-standing and deep regard for Margaret De Patta's work—indeed, all this work may be a mature homage to her jewelry and its importance to him throughout his development. *Satellite* harks back to those Modernist pieces of De Patta's he saw in the Oakland Museum as an undergraduate. De Patta's *Pin* (1944) may be the basis for *Satellite*, with Cory quoting it both in composition—note how similarly he treats the placement of the stone, the overall fluidity of the mass and its parts—and in concept: jewelry as sculpture, not simply decoration. *Satellite* is technically stunning in the way he's treated the

(Untitled) Rope (pin), 1971
Cast copper, silver, brass, and plastic
1½ × 1½ × ½ in.
Whereabouts unknown

Satellite (aka **Orbit**) (pin), 1991
Silver and carnelian
2¼ × 1¾ × ⅜ in.

Fire (pin), 1988
Silver, copper, 18K gold, and garnet
2 × 1½ × ¾ in.

Arm (pin), 1988
Silver, copper, 22K gold, and garnet
2 × 1¼ × ½ in.

Dress (pin), 1988
Silver, copper, 22K gold, 18K gold,
and blue topaz
2¼ × 1¼ × ½ in.

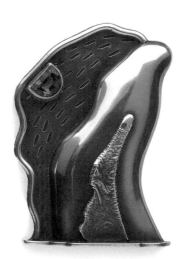

Landscape (pin), 1988
Silver, 22K gold, and tourmaline
2 × 1¼ × ½ in.

Architecture (pin), 1987
Silver, 18K gold, and lapis
2 × 1¼ × ½ in.

Knows (pin), 1991
Silver and garnet
1⅛ x 2 x ½ in.

surface, the subtle variation of texture, the way light plays differently on the two sides, and the surface contrasts of those two arches that loop down below the solid mass.

There are so many other dynamic pairings here: the 1987 *Architecture* and its relationship to Cory's early *Window*, and to the pueblo architecture he saw throughout his life on the summer road trips. The number 5 used in *Coffee*, *Boat*, and *Sign*. The early *Nipple* and the late *Knows*. *Dress* and its linkage with so much of the imagery in Pencil Brothers pieces. The list here could go on.

From the beginning, Cory saw jewelry as a wide-open arena for expression, a receptacle for *meaning*, not merely another form for decoration. He knew, and he knew this deeply, that trash (and that includes the everyday world of common objects), machines and their potentially beautiful workings, the mysterious and sensual resonances of the natural world, and the sexual tensions between men and women were all full of potential because in those objects and in those places there is no sentiment, no pretense.

Free of the commentary of narrative and of the obsession to include the overtly functional, the recognizable everyday object, layers of social content, these last works are visually and conceptually both simpler and more complex than his early work. If art is indeed a language, as Cory knew it was, the last pins possess, like poems, a purity of diction, a consciousness of phrase, a concentrated singleness of affect. He has sifted through all those years of accumulated personal and cultural images and icons, and in the last work has pared down, sorted through the baggage, done the research, and arrived at his most powerful visual/

(Untitled) Nipple (pin), 1967
Electroformed copper and plastic
1¼ × 1¼ × ½ in.

object language by using less, and by refining both the images and the dialogue. These works have a technical and material force that is no longer *fundamentally* ironic or satiric or funny—though that's all still there pulsing under the surface.

Instead, there is a representation, with the precision, force, and power of authentic discovery. The surfaces, infused with feeling, beauty, and mystery, are only the other side of essence. The objects that he loved and studied so deeply have been fully transformed into something new, to him and to us, and to the craft, through the alchemy of aesthetics.

These last pieces speak to us in the pure, hard-earned language of form. A harmony has been achieved.

(Untitled) Beach (pin),1993
Silver, copper, and 18K gold
1½ × 1¾ × ½ in.

Epilogue

It is modest of the nightingale not to require anyone to listen to it; but it is also proud of the nightingale not to care whether anyone listens to it or not.

—Søren Kierkegaard

Kierkegaard was talking about genius. Ken Cory's life and work are marked by that modesty and pride. He never wavered from his belief that art is communication, not commerce. He didn't finish his life's work—but art is never finished anyway, it is just another dialogue with ourselves and with each other. He knew this, from very early on. As he said in the first artist statement we know of, from sometime in the early 1970s:

> In my jewelry, I am translating into contemporary visual language the thoughts of ancient cultures, which are of course the same thoughts we are thinking today. I make jewelry for the same reasons the Egyptians built pyramids, the Alchemists worked in their laboratories, and the Chinese wrote the *I Ching*. . . . The artist's function is not to produce objects, but he produces objects as a demonstration or communication of his spiritual awareness.

Essay Notes

The story told here is primarily an oral history; Ken Cory's family, friends, and peers all survived him. Thanks are due to all who generously contributed the gifts of their memories and stories: Beverly Cory, Nancy Worden, and Les LePere, who made the exhibit and catalogue possible; and Merrily Tompkins, Victor and Bobbie Moore, Ruth Tamura, Jan Brooks and Lane Coulter, Gary Noffke, Linda Watson-Abbott, Ramona Solberg, Mary Lee Hu, Kiff Slemmons, Frank Samuelson, Charlie King, and Jane Orleman and Dick Elliott.

Thanks, though too small a word here, are also due to Paul Hoornbeek and Sigrid Asmus, gifted editors, and to Barbara Johns for belief, insight, and guidance.

1. All the stories which follow, in all the different voices, are drawn from extensive interviews, telephone conversations, recorded dialogue, and documents provided by Cory's family, friends, former students, and colleagues.

2. Two of the best surveys of postwar West Coast and Bay Area art are Thomas Albright's seminal *Art in the San Francisco Bay Area 1945–1980* and Rebecca Solnit's *Secret Exhibition*. Sadly, neither text considers either the crafts or metalsmithing in any depth. My brief overview of the postwar years here is a miniaturized and shrink-wrapped synopsis based upon Solnit's excellent research. See also Peter Selz, *Funk*; and *The California Dream*, edited by Dennis Hale and Jonathan Eisen, especially Chapter IV; and "The Beat Agenda" feature in *Artweek*, October, 1996, pp. 13–20.

   Three chapters in Jonathan Fineberg's *Art Since 1940: Strategies of Being* are also especially helpful for a fuller understanding of these issues: Chapter 7, "The Beat Generation: The Fifties in America"; Chapter 9, "The Landscape of Signs: American Pop Art 1960 to 1965"; and Chapter 10, "In the Nature of Materials: The Later Sixties."

   One additional note: For useful background on American culture in the years preceding midcentury, there is perhaps no more thorough overview than T. J. Jackson Lears' *No Place of Grace: Antimodernism and the Transformation of American Culture 1880–1920*. Lears' scholarship, indispensable to an understanding of American culture and the place of the arts in our society, informs much of my work here.

3. Solnit, p. 27.

4. Solnit says (p.29), "For all that has been written about abstract expressionism at the California School of Fine Arts, it didn't exactly spread like wildfire. Perhaps its ideals of individualism and self-expression were taken too literally by students such as Jeremy Anderson and Jess. . . . Perhaps the Bay Area has never been fertile ground for 'high seriousness.'"

5. "Arneson and Wiley became the hub of a close-knit circle of Davis-based artists that included such students as Steve Kaltenbach, Bruce Nauman, and John C. Fernie, as well as

fellow teacher Roy De Forest. It intersected with such artists as William Allen and Robert Hudson in San Francisco, and to a lesser extent with such Berkeley artists as Peter Voulkos, James Melchert, and Harold Paris. Their work formed the nucleus of Funk art, the most widely publicized Bay Area 'movement' in the middle and late years of the 1960s.

"The best West Coast funk artists created a form of visual poetry, as concrete as its materials and as metaphorical as the connection one could draw between them. They sought to intensify the meanings of their images, and multiply their connectedness with the real world. Theirs was basically an 'outsider art,' closer to nature than to culture, an organic expression of the artists' evolving life and experience." Albright, p. 109.

6. Solnit, p. 29.

7. Albright, p. 81. Together with Solnit's *Secret Exhibition*, there may be no more thorough discussion of the Beat, Funk, and Pop movements in West Coast art than the one Albright provides. See especially Chapter 4, pp. 81–109, and Chapter 5, pp. 112–33.

8. Peter Boswell, "Beat and Beyond: The Rise of Assemblage Sculpture in California," in *Forty Years of California Assemblage*, pp. 66–71. Boswell observes, "No development in twentieth-century art has been more significant than the incorporation of objects from mass culture into works of art. Its [assemblage's] principal role . . . has been to serve as a meditation upon the modern world and its values." Clearly, the assemblage works that Cory saw as a student in the Bay Area, as well as work by Don Tompkins, Fred Woell, and others using assemblage in jewelry, influenced the work he did throughout his life.

9. There is a woeful lack of good scholarship and writing on the history of American metalsmithing and especially on that history examined in the context of the important social and cultural shifts following World War II. My brief discussion here is based primarily on Ralph Turner's *Contemporary Jewelry: A Critical Assessment 1945–75*, and extensive discussions with the metalsmiths Lane Coulter and Jan Brooks.

10. Turner, p. 22.

11. For a gritty and provocative exegesis of this issue, see the excellent and disturbing documentary film *Crumb* (1995), which explores the life and work of the cartoonist Robert Crumb. Though all who knew him well tell us that Ken Cory did not make his work while under the influence of drugs or alcohol, nonetheless much of the new art he saw as a young undergraduate student—Beat, Funk, and the Hairy Who—had clearly been influenced by the various altered states drugs induced in their users. It was a halcyon time.

12. Quoted in Susan Biskeborn, *Artists at Work*, p. 132. Published just four years before Cory's death, Biskeborn's short, excellent essay on Cory's late work is one of the few sources we have in which he speaks about his work. Her essay is an important resource for my work here.

13. Biskeborn, p. 132.

14. Biskeborn, p. 133.

15. David L. Shirey, "Crafting Their Own World," *Newsweek*, July 21, 1969, pp. 62-67.

16. Turner p. 99. He observes, "Even as a student, his [Cory's] jewelry tended to react against traditional aspects of the subject, and in 1968 his work often contained materials that in themselves indicated this revolt."

17. Lee Nordness' *Objects: USA* is something of a touchstone in the postwar crafts movement. Encyclopedic in intention and design, it attempted to create a "who's who" for the American crafts community. Consisting of inadequately short biographies, brief artist statements, and grainy black and white photographs of works, it nonetheless generated enormous attention, bringing to craftspeople and the public alike news of the sea changes occurring in the crafts of the time.

18. Don Tompkins' jewelry, as firmly entrenched in the Pop aesthetic as it was, would seem to be a *likely* influence on Cory. However both Merrily Tompkins and Nancy Worden firmly assert that, though Tompkins and Cory shared a rebellious and adventurous spirit in their work, Cory was, very early, intensely focused upon his own explorations, images, and symbols.

19. Cory's narrative work from this period is an important influence on the jewelry of the time. It is a culturally charged, social, and personal dialogue with both the craft itself and the society it resided in. All Cory's work, even after he moved away from the overtly narrative, had an underpinning of deeply personal, aesthetic meaning. His storytelling—in his own work and with LePere as the Pencil Brothers—forms a rich and complex fabric of symbol, association, mysticism, sly humor and puns, and an authentically regional iconography. Without Ken Cory to guide us, we can only guess at some of the content, origins, and meanings underlying the narrative pieces.

20. The use of the number 5 in American art, compositionally and iconographically, is not unique to Cory and LePere's work. As art students they would have seen Charles Demuth's seminal *I Saw the Figure Five in Gold*, which is based on a William Carlos Williams poem, and Gary Indiana's reference to Demuth's painting, *The Demuth American Dream Number 5* (1963). The Indiana may have been especially influential for Cory, considering the way Indiana incorporates the emblematic, Texaco-like sign in the piece.

21. Biskeborn, p. 135. Kiff Slemmons, who also uses the pencil image in her work, reminded me that Cory's marvelous insight was first quoted in Biskeborn's essay.

22. I first found this story retold in Paul Radin's *The Trickster: A Study of American Indian Mythology* (New York: Schocken, 1972): pp. 19-20. The story recurs in many forms throughout North America and in other oral traditions as well.

23. Mary Hu, Ramona Solberg, and Nancy Worden participated in a roundtable discussion on Ken Cory's work in Seattle in the late fall of 1996. Sitting at a small table covered with his work, from the earliest to the last, the living room strewn with parts of his many collections, these three prominent Seattle jewelers assessed Cory's jewelry, his craft, and his influence. It was clear from their discussion how early they were aware of Cory's innovative techniques and images, and how closely they followed that work throughout his career.

24. The Ellen X. Redheart pseudonym is derived from the name of Ken Cory's longtime home town, the city of Ellensburg. Ellensburg is at the exact (X) center of Washington State, and the city logo is a map of the state with a large red heart at the center.

25. See Kenneth Patchen, *The Journal of Albion Moonlight* (New York: New Directions, 1965). Nancy Worden suggests that this Surrealist novel was highly influential on Cory's work of this time and may be the source for the images incorporated in the revealing paper-weight *Monument to Katie Moon*. The *Monument*, though sharing some of the assemblage-like aesthetic and symbol-laden narrative energy of some other Cory works, is really quite unlike anything else he made at this time or thereafter.

26. See *Craft Horizons* (November/December 1967), p. 26. This is likely the issue Brooks refers to, though Cory also appeared in *Craft Horizons* again two more times—July/August 1968 and August 1970—in this same period. These are very early appearances for so young a craftsman—and a Westerner as well, far from the centers of metalsmithing in New York, Boston, Philadelphia, and Cranbrook (Michigan)—in a journal with a wide national reach.

27. Jane Orleman and Dick Elliott's home, called *Dick and Jane's Spot,* along with Victor Moore's "Castle," are two of the inland Northwest's most prominent and regularly visited "outsider" art sites. Though *Dick and Jane's Spot,* on 9th Street in downtown Ellensburg across from the Police Station, was in its infancy in the late 1970s and early 1980s, today it is a visually rich garden full of whimsical sculpture, found objects, and flowers. Cory, along with other WSU graduate students, helped Victor Moore build his "Castle" (on a hill just a bit south and west of Moore's home, outside Pullman) as Moore's M.F.A. thesis exhibition.

28. Though there are just under two dozen last pins dating from this period, not all of them are equally successful. I focus on a dozen or so here. It is still an enormous output for so short a period of time.

29. See Matthew Kangas, "Ellensburg Funky," *Metalsmith*, Fall 1995, p. 17. This small and important essay, covering the work of Cory, Don and Merrily Tompkins, Nancy Worden, and Ed Wicklander, is a short, concise history of the migration of Funk from the Bay Area and Davis into the Northwest, including centers as far east as Boise, Missoula, and Bozeman, and an overview of Funk's power in the sculpture and metal departments at Central Washington University. Regarding Cory, it is a little right and a little wrong. "Again and again," Kangas writes, "Cory went far beyond the witty illustrations in his collaborations with Les LePere, the *other* Pencil Brother. The C.W.U. professor evolved an erotic vocabulary of male imagery: phalluses, auto parts, urinal traps, spark plugs and batteries. These were executed in exquisitely intricate *feminine* techniques, however, like champlevé and cloisonné enamels. A late work like *Tent Brooch* [now called simply *Tent*] retains all the mystery of Ellensburg Funky (insect? switch? vagina?) yet demonstrates a refined feeling for silver stamping, gold accents, and a single carnelian stone."

First, no. Those Pencil Brothers pins, buckles, ashtrays, and switch plates are always more than merely witty illustrations; they are a caustic, often vulgar, more often hilarious, incisive social and cultural narrative, an ongoing dialogue with consumer culture and the decorative arts, a brawl with the hegemonies of contemporary art. Second, yes, Cory's last works retain the mystery of Funk, and demonstrate a "refined feeling" for traditional craft, but no, they are no longer Funk at all. The problem here is that the Funk label fits Cory's work only up to 1986, perhaps only up to the early 1980s. Funk, applied to Cory's whole career and vision, is a critic's ghetto, an empty label, a reductionist and debilitating shorthand which fails to fully understand the last work.

See also Helen W. Drutt English and Peter Dormer, *Jewelry of Our Time: Art, Ornament and Obsession*. The book is monumental—you could rest your axle on it for a tire change—and represents an enormous amount of research on the editors' part. Regarding Cory's work, the editors say: "To state that a section of American jewelry is a form of new folk art is, in some company, to consign the work to the second division. But in the jewelry of Don Tompkins, Merrily Tompkins, Woell and Cory there is an approach to contemporary culture that does not exist in Europe, and that is as conceptually interesting as it is emotionally affecting." (p. 29.) The conceit doesn't quite work. Folk art will, regardless of the vagaries of the commercial market, always be considered lesser than the "fine arts and fine craft," and no amount of protesting—that "but" up there just doesn't do it—can address the deeper issue at work here. Cory, even seen as part of the Funk movement he came out of and moved beyond, was never a folk artist in the first place, consigned or not. The earliest Beat, Pop, and Funk artists, and then their followers (which include Ken Cory), mined American consumer culture for potent visual, political, and intellectual content and then formed that content into a highly sophisticated, socially savvy, cultural dialogue which forced the art community to reckon with their own specific brand of regionalism and personal iconography.

Ben Mitchell, Director of the Sheehan Gallery at Whitman College, Walla Walla, Washington, is a writer and curator. He lives in northeast Oregon's Blue Mountains.

The House

Ken Cory's house was his laboratory. On the northwest edge of town very near the university, it is tiny, just six small rooms on one floor and a basement he used for storage. One entered from either the front or the side doors, where he had posted enameled signs he'd made that read *"NO Peddlers, Solicitors, Missionaries, Politicians."* The sign on the side door is still there today. The kitchen was carefully papered with Stokely Van Camp's Pork and Beans can labels that Cory and Les LePere found spilled out of a truck wreck one winter night on Interstate 90 outside Ellensburg. Off the kitchen is a small room, one of his studios, and his living room where in later years he had his large, overstuffed chair; the wonderful table he built; a big, boxy gas heater—the only ugly thing in the house—with an old

Front view of Ken Cory's house, Ellensburg, 1994

enameled "Western Union" sign affixed to its side; a daybed which served as a couch; a wooden rocking chair; and not much else of comfort. Friends said it was awfully hard to get comfortable in that living room unless you got the big chair. From the living room there is a narrow hall leading to two other small bedrooms, one of which served as another studio and office, and at the far end the bathroom, not much wider than the width of two toilets, and the only room with a door.

Throughout the house were displayed his collections, in part or whole. In the living room at the time of his death in 1994, there were the miniature cast-iron frying pans he loved so much ringing a wall of boxes containing the dozens of nooks in which he displayed his bottles or toys or antique jewelry; on another wall there was a second group of boxes housing more tiny objects; he had a large collection of Columbia Plateau Native American beaded baskets displayed on the wall of his bedroom; over the tub in the bathroom there was a large, round, antique enameled Texaco gas station sign, and above that a small stained glass window he had installed. Throughout the house there were old game boards, folk art signs, bottles of used pencils—literally hundreds and hundreds of objects, most of them miniature things.

The front room, with collection boxes on east wall, 1994

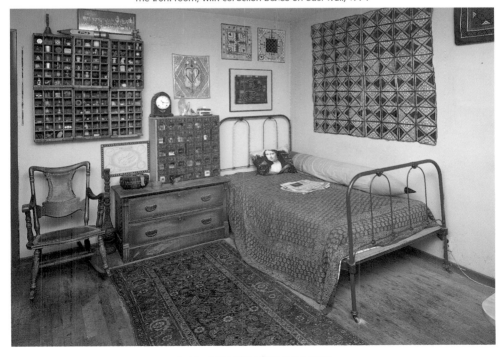

Another view of the front room, 1994

The house, in reality a series of studios, was neat, everything in it carefully and intentionally placed—tools and the workbenches in the metalsmithing studios, his bed in the bedroom covered with an old quilt, the thoughtful display of objects and signs, the collections. Nearly *everything* in the house served as his research for jewelry, for technical exploration and experimentation, for his life-long study of the object—in the form of commercial, cultural, and personal symbols and images. A *personal* study.

One of Ken Cory's enamel door signs, ca. 1970s
Collection of Nancy Worden

Sometime in the late 1970s some of his students stole a wooden railroad crossing sign and left it in his front yard. Later— Susan Cory told this story to Merrily Tompkins—Cory and his mother planted it in the front yard while his father looked on in horror. It is there today. He brought several trees up from the California Coast range, including redwood seedlings, and planted them in the yard. They thrive there today. The house was sided with ugly, green, old-fashioned asbestos shingles when he first rented it, sometime in the early 1980s; after he bought it he finished the exterior with lovely unstained cedar shakes. There is a large backyard where a massive, open-grown elm tree grows close to and spreads over the house. His MG was parked under a frayed tarp by the back fence.

His was the home of a man who lived and worked alone. It was the only Ellensburg house he lived in.

Gaston Bachelard's *Poetics of Space*, a rare and beautiful philosophical exploration of the various kinds of space that kindle the imagination, offers a doorway (even though a very small crack, a doorway nonetheless) to understanding scale— miniaturization—in Ken Cory's work. Reading Bachelard, I also sensed the importance of both Cory's collecting and the house itself, and the fundamental role they played in his art:

> [The] house breathes. First it is a coat of armor, then it extends *ad*
> *infinitum*, which amounts to saying that we live in it in alternate
> security and adventure. It is both cell and world. (p. 51)

In the kitchen, with bean-label wallpaper, looking toward the studio, 1994

The bedroom, with examples of Cory's Native American beaded bag collection, 1994

To understand his house—the way he lived there, its function as a sanctuary and as a laboratory, as a repository for all his collections, for his tools and machines and materials, for the deep visual and technical research he devoted his life to—is to understand his life and work as a kind of poetry, a poetic inquiry.

> The cleverer I am at miniaturizing the world, the better I possess it. But in doing this, it must be understood that values become condensed and enriched in miniature. Platonic dialectics of large and small do not suffice for us to become cognizant of the dynamic virtues of miniature thinking. One must go beyond logic in order to experience what is large in what is small. . . . (p. 150)

"To experience what is large in what is small. . . ." Throughout his life, Cory approached his jewelry as sculpture, creating the monumental in the miniature, celebrating the *essence*, the hidden, and the potential *meaning* of the object in our lives.

> In such imagination as this, there exists total inversion as regards the spirit of observation. Here the mind that imagines follows the opposite path of the mind that observes, the imagination does not want to end in a diagram that summarizes acquired learning. It seeks a pretext to multiply images, and as soon as the imagination is interested by an image, this increases its value. (pp. 151–52)

Cory's essential work isn't the pins and buckles and necklaces and ashtrays, it is his sifting through both his own and the culture's images and seeking a way to understand, to communicate those images through craft, as a kind of shared language.

> Thus the minuscule, a narrow gate, opens up an entire world. The details of a thing can be the sign of a new world which, like all worlds, contains the attributes of greatness.

> Miniature is one of the refuges of greatness. (p. 155)

Ken Cory's work was his life, his life his work. The house he created around himself was sanctuary, laboratory, cell, world.

—B. M.

Tools, workbench, and supplies in the main studio, 1994

Home office, 1994

Sketchbooks
and Artist's
Notes

The sketchbooks are a journal of Ken Cory's visual thinking and research. There were thirty-two in all, including a numbered set of twenty-five—though Number 25, the last, has only five pages of work in it. After he died, more were found in his house, all empty, numbered, and ready to use. They are amazingly consistent, almost all the same size, same brand. He worked only on the right-hand pages. There is very little writing in them, save the occasional singular word, odd phrase (*the domino theory in Northwest metal*), pun (*neo neanderthal*), mathematical tinkering, or calligraphic title (late in his career Cory taught calligraphy at CWU when the enrollments were dropping for metalsmithing). An indispensable record and history, a key to understanding his work, the sketchbooks were a workplace where he experimented with design ideas for his finished works.

The sketchbooks are a key resource for understanding his enduring relationship to the object, to those talisman-like shapes and repeated images which recur in the jewelry. Ken Cory simply loved things, especially small things, and so it is not surprising that his sketchbooks are essentially a lifelong collection, a repository, of hundreds and hundreds of thumbnail sketches, design ideas, and close observations of those essential images he explored.

—B. M.

Development Sketches

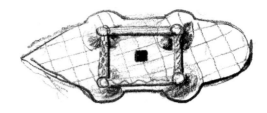

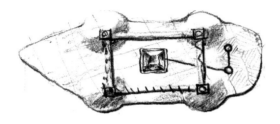

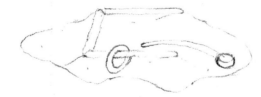

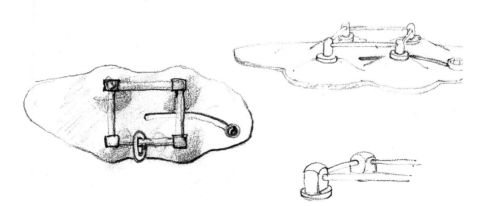

Development sketches for **Boat**. Top left and right, Sketchbook No. 17, 1985;
center and bottom, Sketchbook No. 20, ca. 1986–87.

Development Sketches

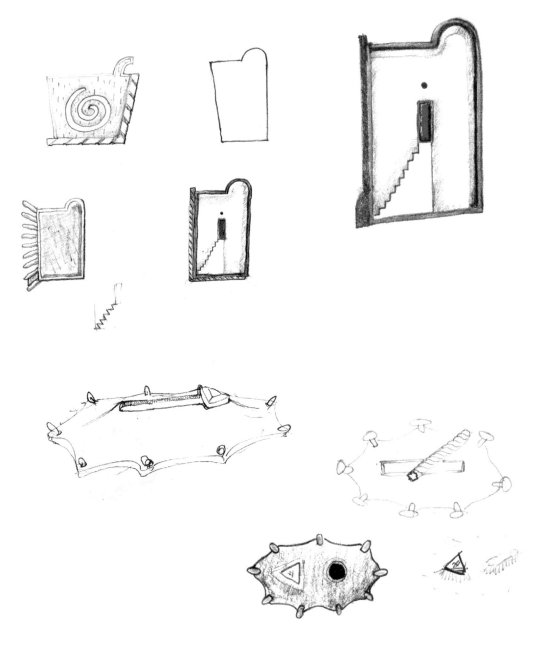

For **Architecture:** top left and right, Sketchbook No. 20, 1987 and far right, Sketchbook No. 21, 1987.
For **Tent**: left, Sketchbook No. 16, 1984; right and bottom, Sketchbook No. 13, ca. 1981–82.

Early Sketches

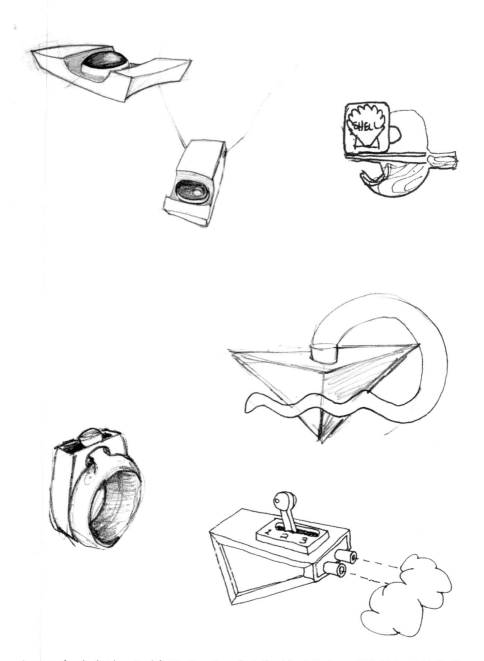

A group of early sketches. Top left, "Mo Derne" pendant, Sketchbook No. 1, ca. 1963–64; top right, **Shell**, Sketchbook No. 1, ca. 1966; center right, **Pin**, unnumbered sketchbook, ca. 1969; bottom left, **Ring**, unnumbered sketchbook, ca. 1969; and bottom right, **Shift**, unnumbered sketchbook, ca. 1969.

Miscellaneous Sketches

Top left, sketch for **Autumn Sunset**, Sketchbook No. 6, 1975; top right, Fire hydrant, Sketchbook No. 7, 1976; bottom left, Ink bottles, Sketchbook No. 16, 1984; bottom right, Post puns, Sketchbook No. 4, 1973.

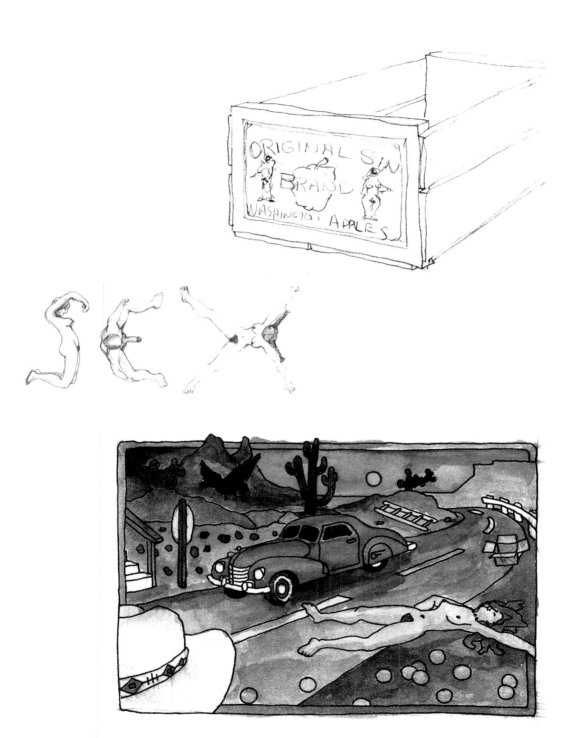

Top: Fruit box label, Sketchbook No. 6, 1975; center, Human letters, sketchbook No. 16, 1984; bottom, complete drawing for **Route 66**, Sketchbook No. 7, 1975–76.

ESSENTIAL IMAGES

JEMS IN DASH

~~SNAKE~~	LOCK	90 ~~BEAVER~~
~~BIRD~~	~~CHAIR~~	91 ~~CAMEL~~
~~ROPE~~	. COIN - MONEY $	92. CONCH SHELL
• STICK	• PICTURE \ PIG BANK	SPOON
~~HOUSE~~	~~WINDOW~~	~~BALL~~
FENCE	DOOR	~~LADDER~~
• TREE	BOOK	~~_____~~
.• VOLCANO	~~BELL~~	♂ MELON
CAR	~~BALANCE SCALE~~	HAT
• RAINCLOUD	RADIO (TV)	~~HAIRS~~
~~TUNNEL~~	THERMOMETER	SHOE
◦ ~~SUN~~	~~ARROW~~	~~_____~~
• ~~MOON~~	◦ RAM	INDIAN
SPECTRUM (SET)	~~ALPHABET - NUMBERS~~	~~_____~~
~~PATTERN~~	COMPASS (2)	
• MAN	PENCIL	PITCHER
WOMAN	RUG - ~~_____~~	FLOWER POT
•. LOG	CHEST OF DRAWERS	104 UMBRELLA
CAT	~~ANVIL~~ ~~HAMMER~~	WAGON
.• FIRE	MAGNIFIER NAILS	▪ MOUNTAIN
KNIFE - SWISS ARMY	~~PAINT~~ ~~CLOTHSPIN (S)~~	JEWEL
RING	SHOVEL	▪ ROAD
. TREASURE	SAW -~~EYE~~	▪ RIVER
TRAIN TARGET	ERASER BUTTON	◦ LAKE
MIRROR TOY	TELEPHONE TOILET	AIRPLANE
~~LETTER~~ GRAIN ELEV.	~~LETTER~~ RUBBER STAMP	~~_____~~
KEY TELESCOPE	COMB	~~_____~~
BED MICROSCOPE JACK	CITY JAX	FRY PAN
• FLOWER FAUCET	CAMERA 8 BALL	~~_____~~
VASE - BOTTLE	• FISH LANDSCAPE	~~_____~~
BOX	◦ HAND PUZZLE	~~_____~~
~~STAR~~	• NUT • STUMP	COFFEE POT
HEART	~~DRUM~~ THERMOMETER	MAILBOX
• LIGHTNING	◦ ROCK SISSOR	UNICYCLE
MAP	~~TELEPHONE POLE~~ FRUIT	BROOM
~~CROWN~~	DUMP MUSHROOM	BOWL
~~BRIDGE~~	•◦ WIND PACKAGE	BUCKET
~~SKULL~~	DICE BERRIES	TRUCK
TOWER	◦ MERMAID LIGHT BULB	LIGHT HOUSE
40 WATER ANGEL	CHAOS TENT (TEPEE)	▪ ROOSTER
CUP	BEADS WHISTLE	BOAT
~~X-ING (R.R)~~	~~JACK-O-LANTERN~~ BEETLE	↳ ZEBRA
~~CLOCK~~	~~PARROT~~ ICE CREAM CONE	
	~~CANDLE~~ WORLD GLOBE	
	FLAG	
	EGG (DECORATED)	

Artist's Statement

My jewelry is first of all sculpture. My primary concern is the idea behind the piece. Design follows idea. My sculptures are not made to decorate the body but, because of their size, they may be conveniently displayed on the body. The pieces are functional only to the extent that they are not heavy to wear, there are no sharp points to stab the wearer, and they are durable.

Too many jewelers let concept suffer in favor of function. My jewelry is sculpture complete in itself wherever it is displayed. It can be worn by men or women. It can be hung on the wall. Small portable sculptures. Too many artists think importance and volume are directly proportional.

All people throughout all time have thought basically the same thoughts. They have been aware of the same mysteries and the same magic. As their environments vary, their languages vary. We have a visual language as well as a verbal one. In my jewelry I am translating into contemporary visual language the thoughts of ancient cultures which are, of course, the same thoughts we are thinking today. I make jewelry for the same reasons the Egyptians built pyramids, the Alchemists worked in their laboratories, and the Chinese wrote the *I Ching*.

I try to ignore the monetary value of materials. I work predominately in non-precious materials, but I do not ignore the precious ones. Why not set a diamond in plastic or combine gold and lead in the same piece? Traditions should neither be worshipped nor rejected.

I do not exclude from consideration any combinations of materials, techniques, or thoughts. Every teacher I've had said copper cannot be cast. So I tried and found it could be cast. It has limitations. But what material or technique doesn't?

The artist's function is not to produce objects, but he produces objects as a demonstration or communication of his spiritual awareness.

—Ken Cory, sometime in the early 1970s

Glossary of Metalsmithing Techniques

LOST-WAX CASTING: A positive of the form desired is carved or modeled out of an organic material, usually wax. A wax channel and funnel (called a "sprue") are attached to the form and both are then covered by the "investment," a liquid, heat-resistant material, that is allowed to harden, making a mold. The wax of the form and sprue is burned out in an oven or kiln, leaving a cavity where the form was. Molten metal is then poured into the cavity. When the molten metal has solidified in the mold, the mold is submerged in water and the steam from the hot investment breaks it up, revealing the metal casting inside.

CUTTLEFISH BONE CASTING: The soft side of a cuttlefish bone—the same as those provided for parakeets to chew—is abraded flat and a design is carved into it. The bone is also soft enough to accept impressions of objects pressed into it. A sprue channel and funnel are also carved in, connecting the design to the edge of the bone. Another flattened piece of cuttlefish bone is wired onto the first one and molten metal is poured into the channel. Cory used this technique in situations where a rippled effect was desired on the surface of the metal, caused by the patterns in the bone.

ELECTROFORMING: This is the same process as electroplating, but a much thicker layer of metal is built up, sometimes on a surface which is later removed. Almost any surface can be plated as long as it is electrically conductive. Nonconductive materials—forms made of wax, glass, stones, plastic, etc.—can be painted with a metallic lacquer to be made conductive. This is how "bronze" baby shoes are plated. The prepared form is attached to a wire and submerged in an electrolytic solution; for copper plating, this is copper sulfate (copper dissolved in sulfuric acid and diluted with distilled water). The form is connected to a direct current—a rectifier or battery—as the cathode. The anode wire is connected to a bar of the same type of metal being plated, which is also submerged in the solution. The current goes from the anode bar, through the solution to the piece and out, taking ions of metal from the anode and depositing them onto the cathode. The higher the amperage, the more the copper builds in the characteristically nubby texture seen in Cory's early work.

CHAMPLEVÉ ENAMELING: Using asphaltum or other protective material, called a "resist," designs are drawn or screened onto a solid sheet of heavy-gauge copper. The metal is then immersed in acid—usually ferric chloride—long enough to etch cells to hold enamel. The enamel, in the form of powdered glass mixed with just a little water, is placed in the cells. After many firings in a kiln to melt the layers of glass enamel and fuse them to the metal, and filling the cells, the whole piece is ground flush and refired for a glossy surface. Cory often gold-plated his pieces for a final finish.

CLOISONNÉ ENAMELING: This is a method of enameling similar to the champlevé work. Here, the designs are created by using thin, flat wires or small pieces of sheet metal to create "walls" for the cells that hold the enamel.

GRANULATION: The ancient Etruscans excelled in this process, where tiny pieces or balls of metal are fused to the surface of another piece of metal without solder.

STEEL TOOL MAKING: Using old files that he had annealed (softened with heat and slow cooling), Cory carved or etched the surface to make decorative stamps. He also made drawplates, or wire-forming dies, from old truck springs, also annealed and then drilled and filed out to the desired shape. When the forming was finished, the steel was then hardened and tempered with more heat.

TWISTED WIRE: Inspired by the examples of twisted wire in Herbert Maryon's well-known book on metalworking, Cory used his rolling mill and the drawplates to create different patterns with wire. Some patterns are a single wire twisted and/or rolled through the mill to create the design, others are two or more patterns (or wires) combined.

MILLEFIORI METAL: Cory probably invented this process, using the same concept that the Venetian glassblowers developed to make detailed patterns for glass (in Italian, "millefiore" means "thousand flowers"). He began with tight bundles of differently colored metal rods, arranged to form a pattern when seen from the end. These were encased in tubing, and then sliced off in sections. The sections were then laid out in a pattern, side by side, and soldered to a single sheet to hold them in place. The finished effect resembles inlay, and no other metalsmith is known to have used this process.

MASONITE DIE-FORMING: A "die" is a pattern for a particular shape. Cory used a simple Masonite die-molding process. He pierced (cut from the center) the shape to be formed out of a sheet of 1/4" Masonite, measuring 4" x 3". Next, he rounded off the edges of the cut-out shape with a file, making sure it was smaller than the hole it came from by at least the thickness of the metal to be formed. He then glued this shape to another sheet of Masonite. A thin sheet of annealed (heat-softened) copper or silver was then sandwiched between the cut-out shape and the hole it came from, and this die was pressed together tightly in a bench vise, forcing part of the sheet into the shape of the cut-out.

PICKLING: "Pickling" means immersing a piece of metal in a mild acid solution to remove the oxidation or flux (traditionally borax, in paste or powder form, applied to an area being soldered to prevent oxidation) left on the metal by the soldering or casting process. Sulfuric acid diluted with water is commonly used by metalsmiths for a pickling solution.

—N. W.

Selected Exhibitions

1997   *The Jewelry of Ken Cory: Play Disguised*, Tacoma Art Museum, Tacoma, Washington; toured

1996   *New Times, New Thinking: Jewellery in Europe and America*, Crafts Council Gallery, London

1993   *Documents Northwest—Six Jewelers*, Seattle Art Museum, Seattle, Washington

1987   *The Eloquent Object*, Philbrook Museum of Art, Tulsa, Oklahoma; toured United States and Japan

1986   *A Twenty Year Retrospective: 1966–1986: Pencil Bros.: Ken Cory and Leslie W. LePere*, Cheney Cowles Museum, Spokane, Washington, and Whatcom Museum of History and Art, Bellingham, Washington

1979   *4th Tokyo Triennial—International Jewelry Arts Exhibition*, Tokyo Central Museum of Art, Tokyo, Japan

1978   *Modern American Jewelry Exhibition*, Mikimoto and Company, Tokyo, Japan

1973   *Portable World*, Museum of Contemporary Crafts, New York City

1972   Solo exhibition, University of Colorado, Boulder, Colorado

1971   Solo exhibition, Erie Art Center, Erie, Pennsylvania

 The Metal Experience, The Oakland Museum of California, Oakland, California

 Jewelry '71, Art Gallery of Ontario, Toronto, Ontario, Canada

1970   Solo exhibition, Museum of Contemporary Crafts, New York City

1969   *Young Americans 1969*, Museum of Contemporary Crafts, New York City; toured United States

 Objects: USA, Johnson Wax Collection, Smithsonian Institution; toured United States and Europe

1968   *Objects Are . . .* , Museum of Contemporary Crafts, New York City

 American Craftsmen Invitational, Henry Art Gallery, University of Washington, Seattle, Washington

1967   *American Jewelry Today*, Everhart Museum, Scranton, Pennsylvania (award)

Bibliography

Readings on Ken Cory and His Work

Books

Biskeborn, Susan. *Artists at Work: 25 Glassmakers, Ceramists, and Jewelers.* Seattle and Anchorage: Alaska Northwest Books, 1990.

Drutt English, Helen, and Peter Dormer. *Jewelry of Our Time: Art, Ornament and Obsession.* New York: Rizzoli, 1995.

Hall, Julie. *Tradition and Change: New American Craftsmen.* New York: Dutton, 1970.

Lewin, Susan Grant. *One of a Kind: American Art Jewelry Today.* New York: Harry N. Abrams, Inc., 1994.

Manhart, Marsha, and Tom Manhart, editors. *The Eloquent Object: The Evolution of American Art in Craft Media Since 1945.* Seattle: University of Washington Press, 1987.

Nordness, Lee. *Objects: USA.* New York: Viking Press, 1970.

Slivka, Rose. *Crafts of the Modern World.* New York: Horizon Press, 1968.

Turner, Ralph. *Contemporary Jewelry: A Critical Assessment, 1945–1975.* New York: Van Nostrand Reinhold, 1976.

———. *Jewelry in Europe and America: New Times, New Thinking.* London: Thames and Hudson, Ltd., 1996.

Wilcox, Donald J. *Body Jewelry: International Perspectives.* Chicago: H. Regnery, 1973.

Periodicals

"The Craft of the Object: USA." *Craft Horizons* 28:4, July/August 1968, pp. 8–13.

Drutt, Helen. "All That Glitters: GOLDSMITH '70." *Craft Horizons* 30:4, August 1970, pp. 42–45, 69.

Dunas, Michael. "Funk Art Jewelry: Ken Cory and the Pencil Brothers." *Metalsmith* 8:2, Spring 1988, pp. 14–21.

Hawkins, Linda. "California" [review]. *Studio International* (England) 190:977, September/October, 1975, p. 157.

Kangas, Matthew. "Northwest Profiles." *American Craft* 51:1, February/March 1991, p. 18.

———. "Ellensburg Funky." *Metalsmith* 15:4, Fall 1995, pp. 14–21.

Meisel, Alan. "San Francisco" [review]. *Craft Horizons* 37:5, October 1976, p. 44.

Shirey, David L. "Crafting Their Own World." *Newsweek*, July 21, 1969, pp. 62–67.

Skoogfors, Judy. "American Jewelry Today." *Craft Horizons* 27:2, November/December 1967, pp. 26–27.

Smith, Paul J. "Craft Moves Toward Art." *Design* (England) No. 252, December 1969, pp. 34–39.

Standout, Dana. "Documents Northwest: The PONCHO Series." *Metalsmith* 13:4, Fall 1993, pp. 46–47.

Stoops, Jack. "Letter from Seattle." *Craft Horizons* 32:2, April 1972, p. 59.

Waroff, Deborah. "Ken Cory." *Craft Horizons* 30:3, May/June 1970, p. 59.

Worden, Nancy. "Ken Cory 1943–1994." *American Craft* 54:2, April/May 1994, pp. 16–17.

Additional Resources

Albright, Thomas. *Art in the San Francisco Bay Area: 1945-1980.* Berkeley and Los Angeles, University of California Press, 1985.

Alloway, Lawrence. *Topics in American Art Since 1945.* New York: W. W. Norton, 1975.

Bachelard, Gaston. *On Poetic Imagination and Reverie.* Trans. Colette Gaudin. Dallas: Spring Publications, 1987.

———. *The Poetics of Space.* Trans. Maria Jolas. Boston: Beacon Press, 1969.

"The Beat Agenda": with essays by Bruno Fazzolari, "The New Beat Underground"; Pat Leddy, "The Space Between the Beats: Some Aspects of Beat Life in LA"; Meredith Tromble, "A Conversation with Wally Hedrick"; and Mark Van Proyen, "Rat Bastard Review in Two Testaments." *Artweek* October 1996, pp. 13-17.

Boswell, Peter. "Beat and Beyond: The Rise of Assemblage Sculpture in California." In *Forty Years of California Assemblage.* Los Angeles: University of California, Los Angeles, Wight Art Gallery, 1989.

Cardinale, Robert. "A Decade of Metalsmithing in the United States: 1970-1980." *Metalsmith* Fall 1980: pp. 23-33.

Cardinale, Robert, and Hazel Bray. "Margaret De Patta: Structural Concepts and Design Sources." *Metalsmith* April, 1983: pp. 11–15.

Chadwick, Whitney. "Narrative Imagism and the Figurative Tradition in Northern California Painting." *Art Journal* 45:309–14, Winter 1985.

Choate, Sharr. *Creative Casting.* New York: Crown Publishers, 1966.

Clearwater, Bonnie. *West Coast Duchamp.* Miami Beach: Grassfield Press, 1991.

Cumming, Elizabeth, and Wendy Kaplan. *The Arts and Crafts Movement.* New York: Thames and Hudson, 1991.

Fineberg, Jonathan. *Art Since 1940: Strategies of Being.* Englewood Cliffs, NJ: Prentice Hall, 1995.

Greenbaum, Toni. *Messengers of Modernism: American Studio Jewelry 1940-1960.* Montreal: Montreal Museum of Decorative Arts in association with Flammarion (Paris and New York), 1960.

Gregoretti, Guido. *Jewelry Through the Ages.* New York: American Heritage, 1969.

Hale, Dennis, and Jonathan Eisen. *The California Dream.* New York: Collier Books, 1968.

Hall, James B., and Barry Ulanov. *Modern Culture and the Arts.* New York: McGraw-Hill Book Company, 1967.

Laisner, George A. *A Retrospective Exhibition.* Ellensburg, WA: Museum of Art, Washington State University, 1975.

Lears, T. J. Jackson. *No Place of Grace: Antimodernism and the Transformation of American Culture 1880-1920.* New York: Pantheon, 1981.

Loyd, Jan Brooks. "Strategies for Interpretation." In *Sculptural Concerns: Contemporary American Metalworking*. Cincinnati, OH: Contemporary Arts Center, 1993: pp. 28-32.

Maryon, Herbert. *Metalwork and Enamelling*. New York: Dover Publications, 1971.

McClure, Michael. *Scratching the Beat Surface*. San Francisco: North Point Press, 1982.

Morton, Philip. *Contemporary Jewelry: A Studio Handbook*. New York: Holt, Rinehart and Winston, 1970.

Phillips, Clare. *Jewelry: From Antiquity to the Present*. New York: Thames and Hudson, 1996.

Plagens, Peter. *Sunshine Muse*. New York: Praeger Publishers, 1974.

Raulet, Cylvie. *Art Deco Jewelry*. New York: Rizzoli, 1985.

Selz, Peter. *Funk*. Berkeley, CA: University Art Museum, 1967.

Solnit, Rebecca. *Secret Exhibition: Six California Artists of the Cold War Era*. San Francisco: City Lights, 1990.

Sontag, Susan. *Against Interpretation*. New York: Farrar, Straus, and Giroux, 1966.

Uchida, Yoshiko. "Margaret De Patta." In *The Jewelry of Margaret De Patta: A Retrospective Exhibition*. Oakland, CA: The Oakland Museum, 1976.

Wenger, Lesley. "William T. Wiley: Fall Fashions." *Current* 1:4 October-November 1975, pp. 14–17, 54–57.

Photo Credits

All photographs by Lynn Thompson Hamrick except as noted:

Index of Illustrations

Untitled works by Ken Cory
are listed under their assigned
names.